5 YEARS TO FREEDOM

A Canadian Guide to
Early Retirement

Réjean Venne

Copyright © 2021 Réjean Venne

All rights reserved. This book or any portion thereof may not be reproduced or used in any manner whatsoever without the express written permission of the publisher except for the use of brief quotations in a book review.

Although the author has made every effort to ensure that the information in this book was correct at press time, the author does not assume and hereby disclaim any liability to any party for any loss, damage, or disruption caused by errors or omissions, whether such errors or omissions result from negligence, accident, or any other cause.

First paperback edition January 2021

Book cover designed with image used under license from Shutterstock.com.

Library and Archives Canada Cataloguing in Publication
Venne, Réjean, 1988-, author
5 Years to Freedom: A Canadian Guide to Early Retirement/ Réjean Venne
Includes bibliographical references.
Issued in print and electronic formats.

ISBN: 979-8-57-6543540 (paperback)

Published by Mindfulfamily
www.mindfulfamily.ca

*To Quinn, Mia and Caleb for helping
me find my true purpose in life.*

TABLE OF CONTENTS

Introduction..7

Part 1: Thinking...15
   Chapter 1:
   What is Financial Independance?.................17
   Chapter 2:
   Why Retire Early?...27

Part 2: Spending 35
   Chapter 3:
   Lifestyle Inflation to Lifestyle Deflation 37
   Chapter 4: Don't Budget…Analyze! 45
   Chapter 5:
   Childcare vs. Full-Time Parenting.................55
   Chapter 6: Forget Local… Go LCOL!...............63

Chapter 7: The Costs of Getting Around 73
Chapter 8: Save on Groceries..........................83
Chapter 9: The Discretionary Expenses.......93

Part 3: Saving..105
Chapter 10: Your Net Worth...........................107
Chapter 11:
The Power of Compound Interest.................115
Chapter 12:
Passive Income with Real Estate...................121
Chapter 13:
Investing Outside of Real Estate....................135
Chapter 14: Tax-Sheltered Accounts............153
Chapter 15:
Investing for Your Children's Education.......163

Part 4: Retiring..173
Chapter 16: Identity..175
Chapter 17:
How to Survive a Financial Crisis..................183

Conclusion...199
Acknowledgements...203
About the Author...205
Notes..207

INTRODUCTION

So, what do you do for a living? Uhh...that dreaded question. It wasn't always this way. There was a time when I proudly stated my occupation and important title. I would even divulge some of my key responsibilities with joy if I was asked. I was proud to have a great career. I worked for a prestigious organization and earned an impressive salary with great benefits.

Then one spring morning in 2018, after a sleepless night, Danielle (my wife) and I both informed our bosses that we were resigning. We were obviously nervous about these announcements. The answers we would give to the standard follow-up questions would shock them. Equally shocked would be the rest of our colleagues and our entire social circle. Did we get a better job at another company? Nope. Did we have a midlife crisis and decide all of a sudden to change career paths? No. We were simply retiring... We were leaving the traditional workforce for good.

This wasn't a rash, spur-of-the-moment decision. We had actually highlighted the day on our calendar six months prior. Our announcements were going to be at least six weeks before our actual resignation date to give ample time to find our replacements and to transition. They would also be on a Friday. That way, we would give everyone the weekend to digest the news and we wouldn't get pummeled with questions right away. Although we still got all the questions on the following Monday.

Even the idea of retiring wasn't a short-term decision by any means. We had started putting the pieces together consciously three years earlier and unconsciously two years before that. Our story started in 2013; we were on career trajectories to senior leadership in the corporate and government world. We loved climbing the corporate ladder and had so much ahead of us. We had already achieved some successes in our careers and could not imagine a life that did not encompass our work ambitions. But when we decided that the next step in our life was to have children, our life goals changed drastically.

Fast forward to 2015 and we had started our family and had already enjoyed an amazing year of parenthood. We were in a bit of a rut, a few months after we put our son in daycare. We were in the toughest stage that most working parents face. On some levels, the first year of having a baby is the toughest stage due to lack of sleep. But for many couples, the second year is just as hard. It starts with trying to go back to a normal career lifestyle, all while being responsible for an additional human being. Each morning I scrambled to not only get myself ready, but to also get this other human out of bed, clothed and fed. I dropped him off at the daycare in the morning then commuted up to one hour to my place of work. Danielle went to work really early in the morning, before our son even woke up, so that she could pick him up at a reasonable hour in the late afternoon.

Then after a long day of work, we were frantically trying to make dinner while at the same time, trying to get him ready for the typical early toddler bedtime. On an average workday we only got to spend two stress-filled waking hours with our son every day. That just didn't seem fair. We couldn't imagine continuing to work for another thirty years before we could retire. We hated the idea of having to send our child to be raised by daycare providers.

One evening, while mindlessly sitting in front of the television and our iPads, (our typical unfulfilling end-to-the-day routine), I came across a news article that would eventually change our entire outlook on life and drastically alter our plans. This Globe and Mail article was spotlighting a man named Mr. Money Mustache. Mr. Money Mustache (whose real name is Pete Adeney), along with his wife, quit their high-tech jobs at thirty years old to retire and raise their son full-time.[1] To us, this idea seemed too good to be true. We probably had the same thoughts many readers of this book may have. We followed Mr. Money Mustache's Blog and eventually read every single article he had written up to that point. There were over 250 articles... We quickly realized that this seemingly crazy idea of early retirement wasn't crazy at all.

We were hooked on the idea and started plotting a plan to do the same. We knew we had a lot of work to do. We created a blueprint to a fulfilling life that would cost us less than $30,000 a year. Our quick calculations told us that we could achieve financial independence and quit our jobs within five years. And then, we designed a passive income stream that could provide for our needs long-term. We didn't stop there. We wrote down our plan. It was a forty-page document that read like a business plan you would present to your banker to get a start-up loan. We also stress tested the possible scenarios that could play out. When we were confident enough with our numbers, we executed our plan.

With our overachieving, ambitious personalities and work ethics, we achieved our goal in three years instead of five. We were still in our twenties when we exchanged our high-paying jobs and big-city lifestyle for retirement. Now three years later, this is a decision I have absolutely no regrets about. Once I left the career world, I struggled with the "what do you do for a living?" question. It took two years of officially being retired before I finally got the confidence to just tell the curious neighbour, or the other parents at school our full truth. "Yes, we're retired..." That's when I started writing this book. I wanted to share our journey to a simpler life, without the nine-to-five work schedule.

So, what do we do? What does being retired mean? The short answer is that we are stay-at-home parents who enjoy raising our own kids. Because we are both home, we have the luxury of flexibility, and have time to cultivate hobbies. We volunteer for organizations we care about. We travel so much more, not being restricted by vacation time. We live purposefully.

I hope to reach readers intrigued by the idea of

early retirement but the ones I hope to inspire the most are my three children. Above all else this book is a record of our family's journey and will be a great souvenir to them when they grow up. This book is not about convincing you that you should quit your job at thirty years old. It's not about convincing you to make enormous sacrifices so you can be financially independent. This book is about sharing our story and proving that early retirement is not only within the realm of possibility; it's actually not that difficult to achieve in many cases. If you are reading this book, I can't guarantee that all our plans and strategies will appeal to you. Many may not even be applicable. But I can guarantee that you will learn something from our journey and hopefully draw some inspiration in our story.

Although this book is written from a Canadian's perspective, a great deal of its content is applicable to the wider international audience. This book will explain:
- Why you should retire, especially if you have children;
- How retirement doesn't have to be thirty or forty years away;
- How you can rapidly grow your net worth to be in the hundreds of thousands to achieve financial independence early;
- How to generate and manage passive income;
- How you can live a very happy and fulfilling life

with plenty of travelling for less than $30,000 per year.

The book is split into four parts that represent the main themes surrounding retiring early as we did. In Part 1, I provide most of the thinking around our plan to pursue financial freedom. I provide a brief explanation of the concept of financial independence as well as the key reasons why we wanted to achieve such goals.

In Part 2, I tackle the number one point to address when considering an early retirement plan, or any financial plan: spending. I like to illustrate spending by making an analogy to a burst pipe. When the water (or the spending) starts flowing, you shouldn't focus on mopping it up. Your first task should be to fix the pipe and stop the water from flowing, or at least control its flow. In this section, I first discuss the concept of lifestyle inflation and then dive into how we brought down our expenses to $30,000 (and then even lower) without sacrificing anything that truly mattered to us. I explain how much of what we spend is related to our decisions to go to work and to live in higher-cost of living locations.

Once you truly understand what your spending is or would be in retirement, you have a better idea of how much money or passive income you will need to actually stop working. That is where Part

3 starts. In this section of the book, I first help you to calculate and assess your net worth. Then I explain the power of compound interest to help you grow that net worth. I also share how we created our passive income and how we manage our investments. This section ends with a guide that addresses the issue of saving for your children's future in the realm of early retirement.

Lastly, in Part 4, I explore what life is like after you retire. What happens when you no longer have a full-time job? How do you live a purposeful life and not suffer an identity crisis? I close the book with some helpful rules we followed to successfully allow us to get past the 2020 economic crisis. In light of the 2020 financial recession brought on by the COVID-19 pandemic, many people rightfully wondered if we had any regrets about leaving our secure careers. This crisis proved to be a very good test to our plan and gave us even more confidence in the lifestyle we chose.

PART 1: THINKING

CHAPTER 1

What is Financial Independence?

What does it mean to be "Financially Independent"? What does it give you? Is it some sort of superpower? Well kind of... There are many definitions of financial independence on the internet today. My favourite explanations come from experts who achieved their independence early on. That is also where I got most of my inspiration. Among them is one of the pioneers of the early retirement movement, Vicki Robin. She, along with Joe Dominguez, wrote an extremely influential and common sense book on money in 1992, titled *Your Money or Your Life*. In this book, the authors defined financial independence very simply as « having an income sufficient for your basic needs and comforts from a source other than paid employment ». I love their simple explanation of the concept. They also further state that financial independence has nothing to do with being rich. Financial independence is the experience of having enough — and then some. [2]

So, in a nutshell, financial independence means being able to sustain your expenses with income that does not come from employment. That type of income is called passive income, which you receive with very little actual involvement on your part. In contrast, active income is income you earn actively while working or delivering services or products. Having a job or operating a business are examples of active sources of income.

The best example of passive income is owning stocks in publicly traded companies. This company may be growing, which increases the value of your stocks and it may also be paying dividends, which is the income you receive. The owners and managers within that company do all the managing. You have very little to do with the actual company itself. Over half of our net worth is in stocks and other investments, which generate a passive income for us. I will discuss how we invest and achieve this source of passive income later in this book.

Retirement is a great example of the state of someone who is financially independent. Most people you think of who are retired are probably living off of a pension that accumulated during their working career. The pension is a passive income vehicle that is mostly tied to stocks or bonds via a mutual fund or a fund managed by their employer. This fund provides the individual with a passive income source for the rest of their life.

Another example of passive income is real estate investments. Someone may own an apartment building and the tenants pay them to live there. They use that money to pay the bills, the maintenance and the repairs associated with the building, and the rest is their profit. This money is considered mostly passive because they are not generally involved day-to-day in making that money. There are many ways to own real estate which will dictate how passive this investment actually is. You can choose to manage every aspect, including doing your own snow removal and landscaping as well as handling all communications. This could involve an average of a few hours per week. Or you could choose to outsource almost every aspect of owning a real estate investment and treat it similarly to owning a stock. In both cases, your return is determined by your level of involvement.

I will discuss our strategy for passive income in this book. With our real estate holdings, we were extremely hands-on at the beginning of our journey but have since stepped back a lot. We sold some of our real estate properties when the market allowed us to make a good profit, and now live on a very passive investment portfolio. Today that includes mostly equity and fixed income securities with a single rental property that helps us generate consistent cash flow.

The greatest benefit to passive income is that it continues to produce, even when you are not actively working. You could be on a thirty-day camping trip or just at home relaxing all week, and your passive income will not stop. You do not need to ask your passive income stream if you can take a day off or a week's vacation. You can also be geographically separated from your passive income without asking anyone's permission.

With enough passive income to sustain your lifestyle, you no longer need active income. So, in essence, once you rely 100% on passive sources of income, you are technically financially independent. Independent from having to go out and earn an income day-to-day. Independent from satisfying clients or supervisors. Independent from showing up at a certain time and staying until « it's time to go… »

That is why I view financial independence as a superpower. It's the ultimate superpower. It gives us the freedom to not have to go to work every day. It's a get-out-of-jail-free card every morning and every day.

The 4% Rule
Many early retirees and even traditional financial planners focus on the "4% rule" in order to determine when someone has reached financial independence. The "4% rule" essentially states that you should aim to have enough investments to only have to take out 4% of them every year to cover your living expenses. Another way to look at it is to take your annual expenses and multiply them by 25 and that number would represent how much money you need to retire.

The 4% rule was coined by financial planner, William Bengen in 1994 and then by a further study in 1998 informally called the Trinity Study.[3] The study analysed the US stock market from 1926-1995 and determined the probability that certain portfolios would last thirty years while being withdrawn by specific amounts. Essentially, the authors of the study looked at every possible scenario as a starting point. That even included starting your retirement right before the start of the Great Depression market crash of 1929 (89% drop over three years) and Black Monday in 1987 (20% drop in one day). Under 98% of the possible scenarios with a 75%/25% split between stocks and bonds and relying on withdrawing 4% of their starting balance every year, the investors would never run out of money on a thirty-year horizon. This was while accounting for and increasing (or decreasing) the withdrawal amount to account for inflation (or deflation). Under a 3% withdrawal rate, the success rate was 100%.

Under this plan, your investments would be primarily in the stock markets and bonds. A simpler way to look at this is to examine just the recent past. Even with huge market fluctuations in the last thirty years, the North American stock markets have generated an average of over 7% annual returns. Consequently, even while assuming 2% for inflation, your portfolio should grow by at least 5% on average, per year, after inflation. This means that by taking out 4% each year to cover your expenses, your money should never run out and actually continue to grow.

So, using this rule, if you think you need $50,000 per year to live on, you need $1,250,000 in order to retire. If you need just $30,000 per year, you need $750,000.

As I will outline in this book, we adopted more of a hybrid model of this common early retirement strategy. Although we had achieved a net worth high enough to live on 4% of our total investments when we retired, we opted for an even safer strategy by which we would never come close to using 4% of our assets in any given year. Our plan would keep growing our net worth into infinity. By investing in a mix of real estate and traditional investments (stocks and bonds), we held a less passive portfolio but were on track to earn much more than 7% returns every year. The book will paint a picture of our strategy and the merits of it.

Can you do it in 5 years?
I don't want to sound too optimistic that anyone could retire in five years. The reality is that it may take longer for most people even with all the knowledge in the world. However, it's not impossible and not even that difficult depending on where you are in your life. When we discovered the concept of early retirement, we had a net worth of under $200,000 (mostly all in our home at the time) and in three years we quadrupled this amount before quitting our jobs. We accomplished this by being a little on the extreme side and taking a bit of an aggressive approach to our goals.

Mr. Money Mustache wrote a very striking and simple article in 2012 summarizing how long it will take you to retire.[4] In one of his earlier articles "The Shockingly Simple Math Behind Early Retirement" he does some quick calculations to give you a good estimate of how long you will need to accumulate income to have enough wealth to sustain your spending. The determining factors are how much you earn (after-tax income) and how much you spend; this determines your savings rate. Your savings rate is the percentage of your after-tax income that you save. If you save 100 percent of your income, you have a 100 percent savings rate. Under such a scenario you would have to work zero years as you would already theoretically have more than 25x what your annual expenses are. On the other hand, if you spend 100% of your income, then you can never actually retire and would have to work forever.

If you had a more realistic 40% savings rate (e.g. household after-tax income of $125,000 per year and saving $50,000), then you would need to work for 22 years. If you could get those annual expenses down to $40,000 with a savings rate of 68% then you would only need to work for nine years.

This analysis was overly simplistic and not meant to be 100% accurate. His analysis assumed all the savings would be invested properly and that the 4% withdrawal rate rule would apply once you are retired. It's important to note that your total employment income includes more than just your salary—it should also include pension contributions made by your employer. Therefore, your savings rate takes into account your employer pension as well as your pension contribution. For example, if you have a salary of $75,000 but you and your employer contributed $7,500 to your pension fund or pension plan, you start off with a 9% forced savings rate ($7,500/$82,500) before you make any other financial decisions.

This rough analysis by Mr. Money Mustache won't give you the perfect answer of when you can retire. But I used it here to spotlight a major theme of our financial independence strategy. Accumulating money or wealth is only half of the equation of early retirement. Equally important to your income and savings (maybe even more important) is your spending. How much money do you actually need to spend to have a happy life? As I will explore later on, it may be much less than you think.

That brings us to the last great inspiration of financial independence that I will draw on in this chapter. Another great pioneer in the modern early retirement movement is Jacob Lund Fisker. His theories and longtime blog really reinforced and inspired our strategy outlined in this book. Fisker authored *Early Retirement Extreme* in 2010. His approach to early retirement was sometimes discounted by many as too extreme, but I loved his book. He still blogs today and keeps stretching the concept of frugality, explaining ways that he is able to live off of less than $10,000 per year.[5] In his now famous book, he stresses that the question "how much do you need to retire?" is pretty much standard. Conversely, "how little do you need to retire?" is extremely rare." This highlights that the biggest tool in early retirement is to focus on the expenses. We always talk about how much we need to retire. But as Jacob put it, we seldom talk about how little we actually need. The traditional retirement model puts way too much emphasis on saving rather than spending. Fisker's book puts spending in the right perspective but will likely present too big of a hurdle for most people. This book will attempt to show you techniques so that you can aim more to a middle ground in terms of your savings rate.

CHAPTER 2

Why Retire Early?

Have you ever read a very convincing book and got really motivated on a new idea? A new idea that you really wanted to execute in your life, but soon enough it was forgotten because life got in the way, and you didn't really have time to explore it? This idea was different for us. It was not about changing our life anytime soon or something that would require a particularly large amount of sacrifice. It was just a simple idea. Many people have retired early and made drastic lifestyle changes in their lives before us.

The current societal expectations had us working forty hours per week. We started our careers like most people, with three weeks of vacation time per year, out of fifty-two weeks. Our working weeks compared to our vacation weeks represented a 94% / 6% split, meaning we would only be on vacation for 6% of our lives. Of course, we had weekends off as well, but we never considered those as a vacation. They were more like short breaks spent catching up on household chores and getting ready for the next work week. We could hope to go up to four weeks' vacation after five more years of service, which would bring us to a 92% / 8% split. Being on vacation 8% of the time still just did not make sense to us in the prime of our lives.

The current life plan for most people is to spend the first twenty to thirty years of their children's lives wrapped up in a busy career. Consequently, only retiring once those children are well into adulthood and busy with their own family. We wanted to retire when our kids were young to be able to spend time with them during their most important years.

We came to the conclusion that we had to find a way to enjoy vacations for more than 6% or 8% of the year. A drastic change in our life such as quitting our jobs right away was not an option since we would not be able to sustain our expenses for a long period of time. Our goal was to find a way to adopt a new lifestyle as soon as possible, and we were willing to work on a plan for a few years if we had to. The key was to come up with a plan right away so that we could envision what was waiting for us.

Simply put, the goal was to be unattached to the standard forty-hour workweek with the option to go on vacation anytime, while maintaining a similar lifestyle level. We achieved this with less than ten years on the standard career path. We were twenty-nine and twenty-eight when we quit our full-time jobs.

"In-Person Parent Time" and "In-Person Children Time"

Your working life is typically between the ages of twenty and sixty. Those are some of the most important years in your life where you really define your existence on Earth. You will typically fall in love and create the greatest friendships. You may have and raise children into adulthood. You will also likely enjoy the best relationship with your parents during these years. And unfortunately, in this time frame you will also enjoy your last years with them.

I always want to make the most of every occasion or holiday because I say "life is short". I had grandparents pass away in the last few years. Each time my parents lost a parent, they were devastated. They obviously wished they could have spent more time with them. We all did...

Do you ever wonder how much "in-person parent time" you have left? Or "in-person children time"? You're probably wondering what is "in-person parent time" or "in-person children time"? In his amazing, 2015 long-form article titled "The Tail End", Tim Urban does a visual analysis of the days/weeks/months we all have in an average life.[6] He helps us visualize how many winters he's lived through, how many Superbowls he's enjoyed, how many pizzas he's eaten, and how much of these he has left in his life span. His visuals make it easy to compare yourself in the same context.

What really shocked me was his analysis on his "in-person parent time" that had elapsed. His life situation is pretty similar to mine and most people who move away once they go to college or university or start their career. He estimates that he sees his parents five times per year for an average of two days each. Similarly, during my career years, I lived 400km away from my parents and I was lucky if I saw them that much. This worked out to enjoying my parents' company on average ten days per year.

Urban further analyzed the number of days he spent with his parents throughout his life. And how many days he anticipated having left with some generous assumptions (i.e. His parents lived until they are both ninety). He estimated that for the first eighteen years of his life, he spent 90% of his days with his parents (90% of 365 days per year equals 328 days). That sounds like a pretty accurate estimate for most of us as well.

He compared this number to his current average of 10 days per year visiting his parents. His analysis showed that by the time he graduated high school, he had spent almost 6000 days with his parents, and had only 300 days left until they passed away. He had already used up 93% of his in-person parent time... Think about that for a second... Your number might not be the same, but it really puts things in perspective. If you knew you only had 7% of your in-person time left with your parents, would you value this time more? If you're in your thirties or forties, you may be well past the 95% mark or even into the last 2-3%. Think about the feeling you get when your phone only has 2-3% battery life left...

Tim's article and analysis really stuck with me for two important reasons and was a major motivation to retire as soon as possible. We decided to not accept the status quo and to change the equation in our favour.

1. Parents
I am lucky to still have my parents. But with a

busy career, limited vacation time and living so far away, I didn't spend as much time with them as I would have liked. If I continued working a regular career and living a long distance away, I would probably only see them seven to nine times per year. I was in a similar position as Tim and was already in the last 5-7% of my remaining in-person time with them. Now that I am retired, I live within ten kilometers from my parents, so I see them much more often. I am also not tied to a regular job, so I am able to easily double or triple my annual in-person parent time. The best part is that I can enjoy time with them while they are in very good health as well. My kids will also spend so much more time getting to know these special people in the best years of their lives.

2. Children

If 93% of our in-person parent time is used up when we graduate high school, then 93% of our "in-person children time" will be used up when they graduate high school. That was an even scarier realization for me. We may use up over 90% of our days with our children by the time they are eighteen. For my oldest, that is only eleven years away. I was determined to make the absolute best of the next decade. I was in a hurry to retire. I wanted our nine-to-five to be filled with days at the beach, watching them ride their bikes and camping all summer long.

The same calculations and logic could be applied to any of your close friends or your siblings. You see these people so much growing up but once your working life starts you see them very little. Living away from my hometown, I only saw my siblings during major holidays, and I was lucky to even see my best friends once per year. As humans we put so much value on our relationships. For us, our close relationships with our family and friends are more important than any material object or any sum of money. The amount of "in-person time" we gained by retiring has drastically increased. And the value we put on this time has made us millionaires ten times over.

Our path is not the right path for everyone, and others will have many different ways to achieve their goals. But I hope our journey can give you ideas or provide motivation to reach retirement sooner than you may currently think possible.

PART 2: SPENDING

CHAPTER 3

*Lifestyle Inflation to
Lifestyle Deflation*

Like many couples, Danielle and I met in university and we hit it off. We were both studying business administration and had matching post-university ambitions. We both had the desire to move to a big city after our studies. When we graduated, we moved to our nation's capital and started our careers. At the time, we never envisioned coming back. The big city and good careers were our long-term future. We were going to climb the corporate ladders and conquer "real life".

I got a very good job that promised quick advancement with a big insurance company. Danielle quickly got a permanent job with the federal government. A career that guaranteed plenty of promotion opportunities and a great salary. We were both making over $40,000 a year with very little expenses, and an apartment in one of the cheapest neighbourhoods in town. We would eventually succumb to lifestyle inflation.

Lifestyle inflation is a modern problem or as some would describe, a "First World problem". The phenomenon occurs when you increase your spending as your income goes up. For example, when you get a raise at work and then decide to spend the increased monthly salary on a newer, more expensive car. Lifestyle inflation often prevents people from getting ahead financially in the long run, as their savings don't grow and they never properly address their debts. Like many households of a generation ago and some still today, I grew up in a home that never had the luxury of succumbing to lifestyle inflation.

I recently enjoyed an evening of reminiscing around a campfire. My parents shared stories about the simple struggles of just putting food on the table in the Venne household. My father described one instance when they had just settled into a new apartment with their three children. They had just enough pocket change to go walk to the store to buy a few boxes of Kraft Dinner for our next meal. They couldn't even take the car out since they were not sure if it had enough gas. This was just one story of many that describe the typical paycheck-to-paycheck lifestyle that many families still suffer through today. The Venne family would go on to more financial security, but Kraft Dinner was still a regular meal when I moved out, and the family never once got a new vehicle.

Lifestyle inflation was always around, but it was not as prevalent as it is today. As I will touch on in the following chapters, we seem to confuse necessary and discretionary expenses more so today than ever. Everyone in the family now needs a smartphone and a data plan. And two vehicles in the driveway, traded in every three to five years, is also seemingly uncompromisable. If your SUV has a heated steering wheel, how can you go backwards to a time when you had to steer with a room-temperature wheel?

One of my favorite personal finance bloggers and authors uses a great metaphor to explain the concept of lifestyle inflation. Morgan Housel (author of The Psychology of Money) says "the hardest but most important financial skill is getting the goalpost to stop moving". In this context, moving the goalposts is to essentially redefine your idea of success.[7] You might say to yourself "if I could just get that next promotion and finally afford that four-bedroom house in the suburbs, then we will be happy". But then once you reach this goal, you redefine your success and still want more, which leads to an infinite rat race.

Looking back to our succumbing to lifestyle inflation, we didn't really see it coming. As we both had permanent jobs, society would lead us to think that our next steps would be to buy a house and a new car, and so we did. We saved enough for a 5% down payment and got a $300,000 brand-new house. This was the maximum we could get financially approved for at the time. Then we went to the dealership and bought a brand-new $30,000 SUV. Now that we had a house, we needed to buy all new furniture to fill up the rooms. So, we went shopping, occasionally taking advantage of the "do not pay for a year" promotions.

We got married this same year. We also continued to pursue our career ambitions aggressively. Danielle completed the intensive Chartered Professional Accountants program and received the prestigious CPA designation. I kept studying and gained two professional designations in my field. We got promotions at work. We went on vacations every winter and had our first child in the next few years. We lived a normal consumer lifestyle. Then, when our salaries kept going up, naturally this meant it was time to buy a bigger house. We were always good with savings, so it didn't take us long to save for another down payment and buy as much house as we could afford.

Less than four years after our first house purchase, we were already set to trade it in. We committed to a half-million-dollar four-bedroom house in the suburbs. It was massive and further away from work, which required more fuel and precious time to commute. We also got all-new furniture again.

We had reached the superficial goal of having our dream house. But the craving for the next promotions or next lifestyle upgrades didn't fade. I would go on to spend $25,000 on an MBA program that I completed in two and a half years. We were determined to grow our careers. In less than five years in the workforce, we went from making $40,000 to making over $80,000 per year each. So, in our eyes, we were winning at the game of life. Our goalposts kept moving and we kept aiming higher, but we were not sure if any of this actually made us any happier. We had no regrets at the time. This was the life we thought we wanted. We were excelling at "real life". Promotions, bigger houses, more things... repeat.

For us, having a child was the flashing light that went off in our heads. It awakened us to the rat race we were in. It was definitely the single greatest moment in our lives, as it helped us clarify our intentions in life. As we will examine in this book, once we discovered our lifestyle inflation, we crushed it. We experienced the power of lifestyle deflation. As you might have guessed, lifestyle deflation is essentially the opposite of lifestyle inflation. We discovered that our expenses and lifestyle costs did not need to rise with every raise or promotion we received. Instead, we could actually decrease our spending as our income grew which drastically increased our savings rate.

Use the concept of lifestyle deflation next time you get a raise in salary or fall upon a sudden influx of money. Don't think of what you could buy or improve in your life by adding to it. Think of how you could simplify your life or quicken your path to retirement by removing something.

Think twice, if you are expecting your second child and decide that now is the time to upgrade to that bigger house so everyone has more room. Maybe it is in fact time to change houses, but it doesn't necessarily have to be bigger or more expensive. When your family grows, you have less free time. A larger house may bite into that dwindling free time even further with more cleaning and more maintenance. Worst of all, it might mean more time added to your commute. We downsized to a two-bedroom condo when we were approaching our retirement as this was the best option we could find for a short-term rental. I loved the year we spent in that lifestyle. I had no yard work, no snow removal, half the cleaning requirements. Best of all, we were a two-minute walk from a dozen restaurants, stores and even a cinema. The benefits far outweighed the fact that we had less room to enjoy. It just forced us to be in the same room as each other more often.

When it comes time to trade in your vehicle, think about not taking one back in return. If you are a two-vehicle family, see if your family can go down to one vehicle and rely on public transport. You may actually save time commuting and enjoy reading a book while someone else drives you to work.

CHAPTER 4

Don't Budget... Analyze!

When hoping to retire early, the most important step is to have a plan. You need a plan to figure out how much money you are currently spending and to figure out how much you anticipate spending down the road with no employment income. Your retirement life is going to be a lot different than your working life, so a lot of expenses will not be the same. For us, our annual expenses dropped by more than 60% by the time we retired.

In the next three chapters, I will go over the major spending categories we had and how our overall spending drastically went down. This made early retirement much more feasible. Once you figure out what your annual expenses are, I will move on to Part 3 of the book where I examine how to accumulate and invest your money to sustain your desired level of spending.

When analyzing expenses, it is very important to be honest with yourself. I mean brutally honest. I have seen too many people come up with a number in their mind of what they think they spend, to later find that they were way off. You can say that you never spend more than $150 on your weekly grocery trip and assume your monthly grocery bill is $600 ($150x4). But many times, you fail to take into account the other trip or two per week to the store for things you forgot. Or that massive Costco run every few months when you stock up on $300 worth of groceries. That is why it is important to keep track of your expenses.

Joe Biden famously said in 2008 "Don't tell me what you value, show me your budget, and I'll tell you what you value". This quote really resonates with me to elaborate on our strategy to track money. Or half of our strategy... This quote was used in a different context than personal finance. It was used during a political race in 2008 but the meaning is important. The most important part of tracking your expenses is to reflect and see where your money is going. Once you see where it is going, you can see what your priorities are. Or as the future President said, you can see what your values are. When used in politics, this quote is accurate (a government's budget reflects what it values). If applied to personal finance I would have rather heard "Don't tell me what you value, **show me your spending analysis,** and I'll tell you what you value".

Don't budget. Analyze! We have never budgeted and you probably shouldn't either. That may sound counter intuitive in a personal finance book. But it's the truth. Many personal finance experts will stress the importance of a budget; however, I don't see them as the key to reaching early retirement. Budgets are a good tool if you are over your head in debt and can't keep up with your credit card payments. In such a case, you need to have a budget that will put constraints on your spending so that you can get out of the deep end. Many people are in this situation. But if you are not drowning in bills, and are getting by without too much difficulty financially, you may not need a budget to get to early retirement like us. Most of you who have picked up this book are in that spot. If you are safely getting by financially. If you are making your mortgage payments, paying into your pension and occasionally using credit cards for unforeseen expenses. If you face economic hurdles but over the long term, you are moving ahead financially and are on track to a safe retirement in the next twenty or thirty years when you will be sixty. Then you don't need a budget. You need to analyze.

When you create a budget, you set certain financial limits to each spending category (i.e. $600 on groceries, $500 on entertainment, $200 on clothes etc.) and then you try to stay within those parameters. When you reach your limits during a given period, you are constrained and try to not spend any more in that category. This strategy is destined for failure and guaranteed to impose guilt on you. If you reached your grocery budget by the third week of February but you need bread and milk, you don't have a choice but to "blow" your budget. If your friends are going out at the end of the month and you've already surpassed your entertainment spending, you will either stay home with regret or go out with guilt for blowing another category. With a budget, you set your parameters now and then reflect on them in a few months with almost a guarantee of failure or shame. If you are successful, the changes to your spending may not come until you've tried the budget for a while. When you analyze instead, you can start seeing results right away.

What does it mean to analyze your expenses? First, you need to compile all of your spending for the last month, or three months, or six months (the longer, the better for accuracy). Then, you analyze it to see what your pie looks like. How big of a chunk of your metaphorical pie does each of your spending categories represent. Here are five simple steps to follow:

Step 1: Take out your bank statement, credit card statement and cheque book. Also write down all the cash spending you did (if you can) for the last month.

Step 2: Create a spreadsheet either with Excel or use Google Sheets (like we do) and create a list of all your major spending categories. Here is a list of the major categories we had prior to retirement, to give you an example:

Daycare
Mortgage Payments
Groceries + Personal Supplies
Car Payments
Property Taxes
Travel
Gas (fuel)
Utilities (Heat, Electricity, Water)
Entertainment + Hobbies (Restaurants, Date Nights, Alcohol)
Car Maintenance
Bus Passes
Car Insurance + Registration
Health + Fitness (Gym, Classes, Softball, Hockey, Golf etc.)

Clothes + Shopping
Internet + TV expenses + Cell Phone
Kids' Toys, Activities, Supplies etc.
Home Insurance
Life Insurance
Home Maintenance

Step 3: Tabulate all your spending down to each dollar.

Step 4: Re-examine your lists and be honest. We will all consciously or subconsciously forget certain items that will prevent us from being 100% honest. For this exercise to work, you have to count every single expense, even that $3 lottery ticket or $1 coffee. Do not put a constraint on your expenses, just simply analyze and reflect on them.

Step 5: Analyze and reflect. Repeat next month.

When you analyze your expenses, you will be awakened to some numbers that you find too high and will automatically adjust many of your habits around those without feeling constrained. It is good to analyze your expenses month-to-month, but the most worthwhile exercise is to look back on your expenses for an entire year. That is what we have been doing for the last ten years. We don't reflect or analyze on a monthly basis but simply look at what the past year looked like and discuss if our pie was split the way we thought it would, and if it reflected what we wanted in life. By reflecting year-to-year, we were able to see what early retirement would look like. And now that we are retired, we look at our annual expenses every January to re-evaluate our financial future every single year.

When we started our journey to financial independence, we took out our annual expense spreadsheet and reflected on what our annual expenses looked like. Although we lived in a fancy house, we had two children and two vehicles, we thought we lived pretty frugally overall. Here is what we were looking at:

	Annual
Daycare (2 kids full-time)	$24,048
Mortgage Payments	$18,600
Groceries + Personal Supplies	$7,320
Car Payments	$5,760
Property Taxes	$4,860
Travel	$4,000
Gas (fuel)	$2,760

Utilities (Heat, Electricity, Water)	$2,460
Entertainment + Hobbies (Restaurant, Date Nights, Alcohol)	$2,376
Car Maintenance	**$1,500**
Bus Passes	**$1,464**
Car Insurance + Registration	**$1,410**
Health + Fitness (Classes, Softball, Golf etc.)	$1,296
Clothes + Shopping	$1,224
Internet + Netflix + Cell Phone	$1030
Kids' Toys, Activities, Supplies etc.	$984
Home Insurance	$828
Life Insurance	$660
Home Maintenance	$576
Total	**$83,156**

So, we had a baseline of $83,156. When looking at these numbers to analyze and reflect on them we came to two striking conclusions:

1. 73% of our expenses ($60,402 in BOLD) were in three major categories. Childcare, Housing, and Transportation.
2. Three of our top five expenses (Childcare, Mortgage, and Car Payments) could be

completely eliminated and our #5 (Property Taxes) could be slashed by up to 75%. We will discuss how in the next chapter.

We were able to bring our annual expenses down to under $30,000 in three years. How did we do it? No, we didn't use magic. No, we didn't start finding our groceries in a dumpster. We didn't even sacrifice anything we enjoyed. The next chapters will summarize how surprisingly easy it was, just by focusing on childcare, housing, and transportation-related expenses. Many of which would in large part eliminate themselves naturally. Then, I will discuss the less important variable expenses such as groceries that can also be brought down by almost everyone without changing what they eat or how they live. Lastly, I will touch on some of the discretionary expenses we don't want to give up (and don't have to give up) such as travelling, hobbies, and entertainment.

CHAPTER 5

Childcare vs. Full-Time Parenting

Being a parent is the hardest job we have ever had. It truly is 24/7. A 2019 study by researchers at the University of Warwick painted a vivid picture of how hard the job actually is.[8] This long-term sleep study surveyed almost 5000 new parents over seven years. They found that sleep quality was affected and parents suffered from sleep deprivation for more than just the first three months after a baby is born. The average mother doesn't get back to pre-pregnancy sleep quality or quantity until their child is six years old.

We've all had tough jobs in the past. Some jobs would make us lose sleep for a while to adjust to a new schedule. Or we lost sleep occasionally due to work-related stress. But nothing that would compare to a six-year lapse in sleep.

It's not just sleep deprivation that makes it a difficult job. Overall, being a parent requires more than the average forty hours per week. You also don't get vacation time, other than the few nights per year you are able to find a babysitter. A less formal study, from 2019 to commemorate Mother's Day by Campbell's Soup Company, surveyed 2000 moms on the actual workload of parenting. The results showed that a mom spends on average ninety-seven hours per week on parenting duties.[9] Even if this number is more evenly split with a reliable co-parent, it's still a significant workload.

Today, many families see both parents sustain full-time careers above and beyond the duties of a hundred hour/week parenthood job. We suffered that affliction for some years and it was our greatest motivator to seek financial independence. At the time of writing this book, we are retired in the traditional sense but far from being bored. Parenting is definitely a full-time occupation that is very hard. But in this chapter, I will discuss the enormous benefits of choosing to be full-time parents.

Daycare
By becoming full-time parents, we would no longer require childcare services. Like most parents, childcare was our biggest single expense costing us $24,000 a year. Childcare costs are extremely high in Canada and in particular, in Ontario. According to a study done by the Canadian Centre for Policy Alternatives (CCPA) in 2019, the average cost of a daycare spot in Toronto for an infant was $1,685 per month ($20,220/year) and a preschooler spot averaged at $1,150 per month ($13,800/year).[10] Most of the big cities in Canada reported similar numbers.

Even once children start school, these expenses don't go away. In Toronto, before and after-school care daycares range from $29-$38 per day. This works out to $5,500 to $8,000 plus the costs of summer camps, March break camps, and the various other days throughout the year that the schools are closed. A school-age child could still cost most parents $7,000 to $9,000 per year in daycare costs.

We have three children, so these numbers really awakened us to the potential savings of not relying on childcare. When we put our plan into motion, we had $24,000 in daycare expenses with two kids. This number would go up with a third child but go down once the children started school. So, $24,000 would be a reasonable long-term figure to keep in mind for us. Knowing we could eliminate this category by retiring, we quickly trimmed 29% of our total expenses!

Getting Paid to be a Full-Time Parent
On top of getting substantial savings from avoiding childcare costs, your "parental salary" will see a huge boost when you retire. Yes, you read correctly, in Canada, you earn a salary for being a parent. It's not substantial by today's standards but it will go up significantly when you reduce your income. I am talking about the Canada Child Benefit (CCB).

This program has had many names since the 1980s, but the most recent version was launched in 2016 as a monthly tax-free payment, to help parents with the cost of raising children. The benefit is payable to all low to middle-income households and varies greatly based on the total family income. A family with a household income of $150,000 and two children under six currently receive approximately $330 per month (or $4,000 per year). At a household income of $100,000, the annual benefit with two children is almost $7,000.

It gets a lot more interesting if you become a full-time parent. If your family income is below $30,000 per year, your CCB benefit with two children would be $13,500. With three children, the CCB goes up to nearly $20,000 (at the time of publication). Add to this that most provinces add in their own version of a child benefit and this number gets even higher. In Ontario, if you combine the provincial and federal benefits, you can get up to $1,384/month per child if you are in a lower income bracket. These benefits go down slightly once the children turn six years old, but they continue until they are eighteen.

We did not plan to stop working so that we could rely entirely on government benefits. When we came up with our plan, the current version of the CCB didn't even exist yet and the program was not nearly as generous as it is today. We always make sure that we can continue to live according to our lifestyle even if all government benefits cease tomorrow. We know that is always a possibility when new political parties come to power. That being said, we cannot ignore this benefit that we are entitled to. Being a full-time parent is a legitimate contribution to our society and one that has been undervalued for decades.

Based on our current lifestyle expenses and required income, we can expect to receive approximately $25,000 per year in tax-free payments from the provincial and federal government for our "child raising costs".

At the time of writing this book, we have yet to experience the significant windfall of such an annual amount. That is because our ambitions have been getting the best of us every year and we inherit good problems. My uncle Dan, who is an accountant, has taught us the invaluable concept of good financial problems. These "good problems" are that we make more money than we anticipated. When you make more money than you anticipate, you pay more taxes and you get less government benefits, but you still end up ahead. That is why they are good problems. In our first year of retirement, we still made significant incomes even though we only worked for the first three months of the year, winding down our careers. In subsequent years of retirement, we had to cash out our pensions at valuations much higher than we anticipated, which meant we needed to take out large amounts in taxable payments. We have also been lucky with our real estate investments, which led us to make more money than we anticipated.

Although we haven't taken full advantage of our "parental salaries" up to this point, one of these years we will. These generous programs can offset the lost income of choosing to be a full-time parent. I don't share the knowledge of these programs to say that you should rely on them 100%. But you can definitely take them into account when doing your own cost-benefit analysis of working vs. being a stay-at-home-parent.

CHAPTER 6

Forget Local… Go LCOL!

Our second-biggest expense was the one we had the most control over: housing. We lived in a four-bedroom, four-bathroom, 3000 square-foot house in Ottawa. We had spent almost $500,000 on it. This was our dream home, newly custom built, in a very nice family neighbourhood. The mortgage on this property with a 20% down payment was $1,600 per month. We had owned this house for a year when we came up with our new plan, but had ordered the house a year before that, since it was a new build. Twenty-four months is not a long time, but we were different people with different goals, so we knew we would have to sell it. Living in a big house was not worth a thirty-year career to us anymore. Selling this asset was a difficult decision to come to terms with. We had to accept that our dream house was no longer our dream house. We realized that with real estate fees, it would be very difficult to avoid losing money on this transaction, since we did not own the house long enough for it to appreciate.

So, we found ways to add value to the house. As the old saying goes, sometimes it takes money to make money. We invested $20,000 in the house. We beautified the yard, added a new deck and a fence. We also worked on finishing the basement with a rec room, spare bedroom, and office. We did as much of the work as we could ourselves to reduce our costs. We led busy lives with our careers and we were soon expecting our second child, so we gave ourselves two years to get our house on the market. It only took us one.

We were one year ahead of plan, but we decided to put our house on the market anyway to give ourselves ample time to sell. We gave ourselves eighteen months to sell our house and properly downsize ahead of retirement.

Prior to the hot real estate market of Spring 2017, we hired a good marketing real estate agent who had a staging professional on their staff. We brought our house back to absolute new condition and implemented all the staging advice we received. We spent $2,000 scouring Kijiji and Facebook Marketplace to acquire every chic, trendy piece of furniture we needed. And before you knew it, we had one of the nicest staged homes on the market.

We sold our house for $560,000 within a few months. We owned the house for just under two and half years, so we did not make a significant profit on the transaction. But we did come out ahead slightly. This part of the plan was executed perfectly, because we did not have to take a loss on this massive house we obviously regretted buying.

With the 20% we had originally put down on the house, plus the mortgage principal we added while we owned it, along with the added value we invested with our savings, we walked away from this house with approximately $170,000 in the bank.

We rented a nice and cozy two-bedroom condo in the same neighbourhood until we were ready to relocate. Our new rent payment was equivalent to what our mortgage was, but we had slightly less expenses now, due to lower utility costs and no longer being responsible for the maintenance. We took a breath and enjoyed the rest of the summer. We had now liquidated our biggest asset and had plenty of time to plan for what the future would look like.

LCOL

LCOL (Low Cost of Living) along with its opposite, HCOL (High Cost of Living) are popular acronyms used to describe areas of the country, based on how much it costs to live. The differences between a high cost of living and a low cost of living area are often staggering. In the totally unattainable markets of Toronto and Vancouver the comparisons are just crazy. As of 2020, according to the Toronto Real Estate Board, the average detached home is now worth just over $1.5M.[11] In Vancouver the number is slightly lower at around $1.4M.[12] Then there are the more reasonable cities such as Ottawa, where an average detached home is selling for just $571,000.[13] We were very lucky to have lived in Ottawa as it is comparatively a very affordable city, but still has just as much to offer as Toronto or Vancouver. We liked living in Ottawa but still did not love the high housing costs. It was still multiple times more expensive to live there than in some of the lowest cost of living areas in Canada.

Our aggressive plan required us to relocate to a low cost of living area. Under an alternative ten-year plan, we could have saved additionally and created more passive income to make Ottawa work. But we were in a rush to reach our goal and not married to the idea of living in the big city. Fortunately for us, we also had plenty of roots in low cost of living areas. Danielle and I were both from Northern Ontario and had a few options to settle on.

We went house hunting in the fall and took our time with our offers. We found a vacant bank-owned property with a backyard four times the size of the one we had in Ottawa. This property was in Sturgeon Falls, a small Francophone community where my parents lived and where we already had friends. This house had been listed for over a year with a starting price of over $100,000 that had crept down to $90,000. The house needed a complete makeover inside and out. But the bones were good. With another long Northern Ontario winter approaching, we knew the bank may not want to hold onto the expensive heating bills for another season. We offered $80,000 cash with a quick closing date. With no financing required and a quick sale, we knew we had a good offer. So we stood firm to counter offers. We waited three weeks for them to change their minds and we got the deal.

Over the coming winter, while we were continuing to live our regular lives in Ottawa, we hired my father to renovate the house. He was a contractor by trade and had expertise in virtually all areas of construction. We drove to Sturgeon Falls for as many weekends as we could handle to help out with the project. We invested $40,000 in the house and in the end it was one of the nicest houses on the street. This house would be ready for us when we quit our jobs the following spring.

With this massive downsizing and relocation, we were left with a surplus of $50,000 and no mortgage on our house. We decided to use that money to further invest in rental properties, which we will discuss later on.

In hindsight, we had plenty of breathing room and could have chosen to relocate to another town with slightly higher housing costs. We could have even chosen a bigger house. Overall, we were very excited about our future abode and hometown. However, someone else's plan could involve strictly downsizing in the same town they are in. If we would have insisted on staying in Ottawa, we could have purchased a smaller townhouse or condo in another part of town which would have met our needs for about $250,000. We would probably have added an extra year to our plans to save the difference so that we would still be mortgage free. But this plan is flexible and adaptable to almost any situation.

Find Your Own LCOL Area
According to MoneySense magazine, there are low cost of living cities in every province. The average house price in Sudbury (ON) is $250,000. In Moncton (NB) it's just $199,000 and in Trois-Rivieres (QC) it drops to $166,000. These are all medium-size towns with plenty of opportunities, hospitals, and access to all shops and services. In our new home town of Sturgeon Falls, average detached houses are in the $200,000 range. These averages can be drastically brought down if you elect to buy a fixer upper. As is the case with most small-to-medium size towns, there are plenty of opportunities to find an older property for a fraction of the average cost, if you wanted to remodel it yourself. Another option many elect for is to live in a townhouse or condo which costs much less than the average in the cities.

One of our Ottawa area friends demonstrated that you can even find a LOCL house while staying within the great metropolitan areas of our country. Ben (also a twenty-nine-year-old retiree) chose to remain in Canada's capital region when he retired in 2019. By following and analyzing the real estate market closely, he found a detached house in a great neighbourhood in Gatineau, QC for $240,000 which still kept him within a twenty-minute bike ride to downtown Ottawa.

According to a 2016 study by Statistics Canada, 63% of Canadian families owned their home.[14] Not everyone has a mortgage on their home but another study in 2019 by CMHC found that among people who did have a mortgage on their home, the average amount was $209,570.[15] According to the most recent data from the Canadian Real Estate Association, the average home price in Canada reached a record high of $604,000 in September 2020.[16]

What does all this mean? It means that the average mortgage in Canada is less than half the value of the average house. That is good news. This does not mean that everyone has more than 50% equity in their home (i.e. owe less than half of its value). But it does mean that many people have substantial equity in their homes. Maybe more than they think. If you just have 30% equity in your home and it is close to the national average in value, you may already have $150,000 of potential liquidity. If you live in a city with higher house prices, then your home ownership could be worth well over $200,000. That is the situation we found ourselves in when we decided to sell our big city home.

These figures are important because they can help you realize that you may already have enough savings to eliminate your mortgage. Although most people are tied to a specific city for work reasons, we are seeing a shift due to the COVID-19 pandemic where people will be encouraged to work increasingly from home. This may lead to the possibility of skipping town becoming more feasible. Once you reach financial independence, then you have complete control on where you want to live. With the possibility of completely eliminating your mortgage by choosing to live in a lower cost of living town, you are much closer to that goal.

Property Taxes
Our property taxes in Ottawa were just shy of $5,000 per year. In most big cities in Canada, this number doesn't sound that high. But when we heard of what we could be paying in property taxes by moving to a smaller town, we were definitely motivated. Our new house in Sturgeon Falls had a total annual property tax bill of $1,612. That was a drop of almost 70%. We are not unique in this aspect. Property taxes in Canada are largely correlated with the valuation of property. According to MoneySense's 2018 analysis on the Best Places to Live, there are many communities in Canada where property taxes are under $2,000 per year. [17] You are likely to pay much lower property taxes if you live in a house that is worth less. In exchange, you do lose out on some amenities, but we haven't found much of a difference.

Our higher city taxes paid for the same level of garbage and recycling service as well as the same level of policing, firefighting, and public schools as we receive in a smaller town. In Ottawa we could visit twelve different public pools, twenty arenas, or seventeen public library branches compared to just one of each in our small town. But the one pool, arena, and library we have access to now are all within walking distance of our house, which was not the case in Ottawa. And they offer just as many opportunities for recreation and leisure. So sometimes more is not always better.

CHAPTER 7

The Costs of Getting Around

Owning a vehicle is expensive. According to Statistics Canada, car ownership is the second-highest household expense for Canadians after shelter costs (mortgage or rent etc.).[18] Transportation-related expenses account for 19.9% of an average household's spending. This figure is not that far behind the shelter costs which represent 29.9% of the total. When we analyzed our spending at the beginning of our journey, we quickly realized our true costs of getting around.

We were already ahead of the Canadian average on this line of expenses. Our total transportation costs were only representing 15.6% of our total expenses back in 2015. Luckily we only had one car payment instead of two, as is often seen in many households. Our second vehicle at the time was an older Hyundai Elantra, which we had purchased in cash the year prior. When we started having children, we assumed we absolutely needed a second vehicle so that we could have more flexibility with our work schedules and daycare drop-offs and pickups. Having a second vehicle did offer us some conveniences but there were tradeoffs. We had to maintain two vehicles, including changing and storing the summer/winter tires twice per year on each vehicle. We also needed to sacrifice some of our scarce driveway and garage space to a second vehicle.

One of the first things we did when we decided we were going to retire early was sell our second vehicle, which we knew we would no longer need in retirement. Since it was an older car, it only fetched us $2,000 when we sold it. We now only had one car payment of $480/month on our 2012 Hyundai Tucson, which only had $7,000 left owing on it. This was an easy monthly expense to eliminate. Along with the $2,000 proceeds from selling the second vehicle, we quickly saved up another $5,000 to pay off the other vehicle which zeroed this spending category.

Maintenance and Depreciation
In retirement, we would never have any car pay-

ments. However, we would not have zero vehicle expenses. We decided to still anticipate for vehicle maintenance of $1,500/year. We maintained this forecast even though we went down to one vehicle. Our SUV was nearing 150,000km and we knew it may require additional maintenance and potentially expensive repairs as it got older. Once we had more free time, we were going try to take on as much basic car maintenance ourselves as we could to reduce this expense (changing the tires, brakes, and oil changes).

We also anticipated that eventually we would have to replace our family vehicle. So, we allocated $200/month to reflect the depreciation of our current vehicle. This $200 per month would be put towards the cost of purchasing a new (used) vehicle once ours was no longer driveable. $200 per month adds up to $12,000 every five years or $24,000 every ten years. Based on our lifestyle we felt that this was a safe amount to purchase the used vehicle we would want in the future. Scouring Kijiji or Autotrader shows, there are many used vehicle options in the $12,000 range that could last at least five years with below-average driving requirements.

Any repairs or maintenance on our current vehicle that would cost more than $1,500 in a single year would likely be extending the life of the vehicle. In such circumstances, the additional costs would be offset by the potential reduction in depreciation for the vehicle. For example, if we are putting aside $2,400 per year ($200/month) towards our new vehicle fund and we predict we will need a new vehicle in the next year. Then we decide to make major repairs on our current vehicle for $2,000 but extend its life by an extra year. In this case, our expenses actually go down as we are saving an entire year of depreciation costs by extending its life by that amount.

This is an important exercise for anyone trying to reach early retirement. Everyone's numbers will be different. You may decide that you still want a brand-new vehicle every five years and anticipate a certain trade-in value for your current vehicle in five years as well. In that case, you just need to calculate the net difference you will need in the future and divide it over five years or sixty months. Then put that money aside monthly as your new car fund. Once you have this number you can put it in your spending projections to accurately see what your true cost of vehicle ownership is.

I've seen many people choose to buy a brand-new vehicle right before they retire and anticipate that now they won't have vehicle expenses in retirement. But that is a flawed way of thinking, because all vehicles eventually get old and will need to be replaced. Even if you retire at sixty years old with a brand-new vehicle, you could very well still be driving at seventy years old and be in need of a vehicle. That is why it is important to forecast what your true long-term vehicle ownership costs will be.

Insurance
With only one vehicle, our car insurance premium was reduced to $500 a year. You might wonder how we can pay so little for car insurance? Once you do not owe any money on a vehicle, collision and theft coverage on the car becomes optional. That means you are only obligated to carry and pay for liability insurance. You do take the risk that if you are responsible for an accident, you will not have physical coverage to repair or replace your vehicle (not-at-fault accidents would still be covered). We were comfortable with this risk when weighing our options and the savings included. Our car was not worth a significant amount. I had calculated that the annual savings from declining collision and theft insurance amounted to $700 or 1/10th of the vehicle's value. Since we didn't anticipate being responsible for a total wreck more than once every ten years, the insurance premium was not worth it. It had never happened in over ten years of driving so far, so we were comfortable with the calculated risk exposure of this decision.

According to one study in 2017, the average driver will be in a collision once every 17.9 years.[19] Assuming that in every accident you are involved in throughout your life, you are at fault only 50% of the time, then the average driver would be involved in an at-fault collision every 35.8 years (17.9x2). The additional coverage only adds protection for at-fault collisions as you will generally always be protected even with basic coverage if you are not at fault. We counted as two drivers in our lives; however, we only planned to drive the equivalent kilometers of a single driver, since we only had one vehicle and didn't plan on surpassing 10,000km per year.

So, our math on at-fault collision coverage had us paying 1/10th of the value of our vehicle every year in order to protect us from having to pay the whole value of the car once every 35.8 years. It just did not seem like a good deal.

Obviously this does not mean that there is no possibility that we will crash our car tomorrow and be responsible for the entire cost of replacing it, making the at-fault collision a smart option in hindsight. But over the long term, the statistics lead us to believe that we are better off insuring ourselves. This is only a prudent option when you know you can take on the risks involved. In this case, we know we can handle a one-time expense of $10,000 and our financial future will not be ruined.

The statistics may paint a similar picture on home insurance; however, at this point we are not prepared to take on the risk of having to pay $200,000 to replace our home. Such an expense would have long-term financial consequences for us, so we insure against it. It's important for everyone to examine their insurance options and determine if they have the right coverage for what their risk tolerance is. Another option to save on insurance costs is to increase the deductibles. If you are willing to take on a higher portion of the cost of repairing your vehicle should it be in a collision, you can save on your insurance premium.

Public Transportation
Although not directly related to vehicle ownership, public transportation is also an important expense in this category. For us, even though we had two vehicles, we still used the public buses almost daily. In order to avoid downtown traffic and very high parking costs, Danielle parked at a free parking lot and took a bus to work. Once we left Ottawa, our public transportation (bus pass) budget would be entirely eliminated.

Fuel
Lastly, our fuel budget would be drastically re-

duced in retirement. I worked approximately 30km from home and with rush hour traffic in the morning and afternoons, we were filling up at least once per week. In our new hometown, all the amenities would be within walking and biking distance, and many family members and friends would be close by. Since retirement we have been getting by on less than one fill-up per month.

After the BIG THREE
In the last three chapters we shared how we handled the big three expense categories (childcare, housing, and transportation). When we drastically changed our forecast for these categories and even eliminated some, we came to realize we really didn't have that much spending to sustain once we would reach retirement. This was a bit shocking, but it proved to us that this plan was definitely doable. You may see similar revelations once you analyze your own numbers.

Without touching our other twelve major spending categories, we were already on track to eliminate over $53,000 from our annual spending. Here is a breakdown of our pre-retirement and retirement spending analysis focusing on just childcare, housing, and transportation.

	Pre-Retirement	**Retirement**
Daycare (2 children full time)	$24,048	$0
Mortgage Payments	$18,600	$0
Car Payments	$5,760	$0
New (Used) Car Fund	$0	$2,400
Property Taxes	$4,860	$1,612
Gas (fuel)	$2,760	$680
Car Insurance + Registration	$1,410	$560
Bus Passes	$1,464	$0
Total	**$58,902**	**$5,252**

Savings: $53,650!!!

As outlined in chapter four, we were spending $83,156 per year pre-retirement. Our new projected annual expenses would be **$29,506** in retirement. This was without sacrificing our travel budget, entertainment budget, or our hobbies.

By simply quitting our jobs to take care of our children and addressing housing and transportation expenses, we could bring our annual required cash flow down drastically. But we knew we could save elsewhere in order to give ourselves more flexibility. Flexibility for the unexpected. Or flexibility to spend more on travelling if we wanted. In the next two chapters we will share our strategies for the other variable categories.

CHAPTER 8

Save on Groceries

We were already pretty frugal when it came to groceries. But just like most working families, we still relied often on prepackaged foods. We also didn't always have the time to shop around to make sure we got the best price on key staples in our kitchen. Once we retired, we envisioned having a much bigger garden from late spring to early fall. We would try to eat as much of our own vegetables as possible and try to conserve an additional supply for the winter. In retirement, we would rely much less on prepackaged snack items for the kids and would focus on making our own (apple sauces, muffins, trail mixes etc.). When you have kids, you quickly realize how expensive snack items to keep them fueled can be.

When we started analyzing our spending, we had a baseline of $610 a month for groceries and personal supplies. This represented approximately $550/month ($6,600 per year) on food items and $60/month on personal supplies. When comparing this around I found that we were very comparable to the Canadian average. In 2017, the average household spent $5,934 on food from stores.[20] Canadians also spent a significant amount on food from restaurants, however we categorized restaurants as an entertainment expense so I won't break it down here.

For most households, food is the third-highest expense after shelter costs and transportation. For us, this category would quickly move up to first place once our mortgage and daycare costs were eliminated and our transportation costs were drastically reduced. Our new forecast had groceries representing 20% of our total spending. It is important to not only focus on costs when analyzing food, as some healthier food items can sometimes cost more. But in many aspects a healthy diet can also cost much less.

Once we got through the big three expense categories and groceries would now make up such a large portion of our spending, it was worth a deep analysis. By analyzing our food spending we found many ways to save further and become healthier in the process. In this chapter, I outline the top five strategies that helped significantly reduce our family's food budget.

1. Stores Matter

I can't stress enough how much the choice of where you shop matters. We are very lucky that in our small town we have multiple grocery stores as well as a dependable delivery service like Amazon available all the time. There was a time in our lives when we didn't pay much attention to the stores we shopped at. We figured we paid a little more at some higher-end chains in return for some higher-quality food. What I have come to learn is that the difference in price is not "little" and the quality of food between stores is really not that different.

Some stores have a slightly better selection and fresher produce, but sometimes at two or three times the price. On any given week, you can find staple items such as store-brand peanut butter on sale at No Frills (a Canadian discount grocery chain) for under $3. In contrast, a brand-name jar at a higher-end store such as Metro could be regularly priced at $7. There are hundreds of these examples in each store. That's why it's important to choose a lower-end store such as No Frills, Walmart or Freshco (in Canada). Sometimes you will find that some produce items are of better quality at the higher-end store in your town. If that is what is stopping you from shopping around, I suggest that the potential savings is worth stopping at two different stores. One for your produce and one for everything else. Another solution could be price matching items at your preferred grocer. Many stores now allow you to price match by bringing in another store's flyer in print or on your phone.

2. Buy in Season and on Sale

Have you ever noticed that the cost of apples and carrots are drastically reduced in early fall and cucumbers are on sale in early summer. This is because many items' supply goes up when they are in-season. When apples are in season and all the harvesters are collecting them, the stores offer really great discounts. Gala apples can cost as much as $2/lb during the year and drop to as low as $0.50/lb in large bags come September. Carrots will cost around $2 to $3 for a 2lb bag most of the year but will then be offered in a 10lb bag for the same price come harvest time.

This is the case for almost all produce items. A 10lb bag of potatoes can range from as low as $2 to as much as $4 from one week to the next. These prices are not always reflective of the seasons. Stores just happen to offer different produce items on sale any given week. They may stock up on a certain item in order to offer it at a much lower price. Knowing that every week some produce items will be drastically cheaper, we plan our weekly meals based on what is on sale. This goes for all the items in the store beyond produce. Before making our grocery list every week, we first make our meal plan for the following seven days reflecting the major sale items in this week's flyer. If we want to make a spaghetti sauce, we will use the broccoli that's on sale for $1 instead of the celery that costs $4 this week. If the burritos wraps are on the front page of the flyer at $1 per bag, then we will have burrito night on Monday and Thursday this week.

We never get hooked on a single brand of cereal, crackers, or any other snacks. Every week, there is one brand of each type of product that is on sale and that is the one we buy assuming it meets our nutritional needs. One week a box of cereal such as Harvest Crunch which normally costs $3 may cost $2 per box so we will stock up. The next week, Special K will be half price so that is our breakfast choice that week. The same goes for many items in the store, from coffee to margarine.

3. Stocking Up
When certain non-perishable items go on sale we stock up. When we renovated our current house,

we made sure to build an extra-large pantry. This allows us to store much more food. Stocking up on items you know you will 100% need can save you huge amounts of money down the road. For example, with three children, our family eats so many granola bars. We know that we will be eating granola bars for the next fifteen years and we know that most boxes have a shelf life of one to two years. We go through three boxes of granola bars per week or 150 boxes per year. We normally buy different kinds but generally stick to the same three or four brands which are all in the neighbourhood of $2 per box. If one week, our local store has a sale on a certain brand marking them down to $1 per box, then we can lock in that price for a year if we just fill our basket with 150 boxes. We haven't gone to that extreme yet, but we will buy at least a month's supply knowing there will likely be another similar sale within the next few months.

Keeping this in mind, with the right strategy our family granola bar addiction cost can be split in half. This is the same case for so many other items from soup to canned vegetables. When a certain canned vegetable is drastically marked down, we stock up for the winter months when fresh produce is much more expensive. We also know we will need toilet paper, toothpaste, shampoo, among other personal items, for the rest of our lives. We can safely stock up on at least a year's supply of each of these items when we see a great sale. The billionaire investing genius, Warren Buffet, once accurately said "whether we're talking about socks or stocks, I like buying quality merchandise when it is marked down." When you know you will need to buy something and you get the chance to buy it marked down, it's a no brainer. If half the items in your pantry can be purchased for half the price, then you can save thousands of dollars every year just by strategizing.

Lastly, consider investing in a deep freezer if your family eats meat. By buying meat in bulk and freezing it, you can save a fortune long term. When chicken is on sale for under a dollar per pound, you can stock up to last you a couple of months instead of just the week.

4. Gardening
Danielle and I both grew up in households that loved gardening. Danielle has always had a particularly strong passion for gardening and always kept a small vegetable garden for our family during the early years of our journey. It was mostly a hobby that did not really provide savings but offered some gratification when we were able to eat food that we grew ourselves.

Since we retired, we have put much more effort into this pastime and have turned it into a profitable endeavour. Anyone can make a garden, and one that provides huge savings for your family. It took many years of trial and error, but we have come to find the right fruits and vegetables that we can capitalize on in our climate. Today we have 300 square feet of our yard dedicated to gardening.

Salads such as kale, arugula, and spinach can yield enough for all our salad needs from mid-summer to late fall. We also get an abundance to freeze and make smoothies into winter. The few dollars we spend on seeds are made up quickly, because one container or bag of salad often costs $4 or $5. When it comes to potatoes or garlic, we don't even need seeds. These plants can be regrown year after year using its own harvest. We simply allocate a small portion of the year-end harvest and replant them in the ground to yield a free harvest the following year. One clove of garlic will yield an entire bulb and one small potato can produce six more larger ones. We cook with lots of garlic and would normally buy at least a dozen bulbs per month. Now that we know that a single bulb with twelve cloves can be replanted in the fall and produce twelve bulbs the following summer, we plan accordingly. This plant can be stored and kept for up to six months and can also be canned very well, so we always plant enough for a year's supply. We planted nearly 100 bulbs last fall.

5. Making your Own Food
I have to admit that I aged myself very quickly by becoming a canning enthusiast in the last few years. Canning is a method of preserving food that our ancestors used way more than we do today. Since we have refrigerators, freezers, and the food manufacturers can our food for us, we have less of a need for it. But canning food can still produce some savings on your grocery bill and even help at Christmas time when you have someone on your list who is difficult to buy for. Who doesn't like food? Every year we can our entire harvest of garden beets to make pickled beets. We also make large batches of salsa with garden tomatoes and jam with our strawberries and rhubarb. We get to enjoy these all year and have gift ideas for almost anyone.

Another strategy we are trying to embrace more is preparing snacks. From making our own apple sauces to making healthy muffins regularly. Most of the time when you can make a product yourself, you are likely to save money and end up with a healthier option.

Retirement allowed us to spend more time on hobbies such as gardening and preparing more food items to save money and help us live a healthier lifestyle. It also allowed us the convenience of shopping around more and being much more mindful about our expenses. We are three years into retirement and we have trimmed groceries and personal items spending by almost $2,000 per year.

CHAPTER 9

The Discretionary Expenses

Discretionary expenses are the ones that can go up or down and can be completely eliminated in an emergency. Everyone should know what their discretionary expenses are. As much as we have come to rely on such things as smartphones, cable television and restaurant food, these are not necessary expenses. These expenses are not ones we planned to eliminate, but we did want to analyze them to see if they would be reflective of a retirement lifestyle. We focused on the key spending categories we knew we had a lot of control over. In this chapter, I will go over our strategy to address these expenses. I will also reflect on how our overall spending actually turned out, three years into our extremely early retirement lifestyle. My hope is that this chapter will help you reflect on your own discretionary spending and build an understanding of the key differences between these and the necessary expenses in life.

Entertainment + Hobbies

In retirement we didn't plan on reducing our entertainment budget. With much more free time, we figured we may crave even more entertainment. However, we would have much more flexibility on when and what we could do. At least once per year, we booked a two or three-night getaway at a hotel resort to enjoy some alone time with no kids. This was always done on a weekend and sometimes during peak seasons which costs more. In retirement, we only planned to take these getaways midweek and at off-peak times, which would result in paying sometimes half the price.

We also always know that entertainment is 100% discretionary. Meaning that, if we have a very bad year financially, we could trim this expense. Or we could decide to do a bit of additional income-generating work to increase it if we wanted to. This expense along with all our discretionary ones would always be entirely in our control.

Our hobbies would also be a discretionary expense. We quickly learned that oftentimes our hobbies could cost zero dollars and, in many cases, make us extra money. Gardening was always a passion of ours and we knew this would be an important hobby in retirement. Although this hobby involves some initial setup costs, it generally does not cost anything afterwards and actually provides financial benefits in the form of free groceries.

I really liked golf before I had children and wanted to make more time for this hobby once the children were a little older. I also intended to introduce my children to this sport one day. As opposed to paying up to $60 per round of golf in a big city, green fees were much lower in our new small town. One of our local golf courses had $12 green fees and an annual membership option of only $200. I could also bring my son golfing on Wednesdays for free. I could realistically participate in this sport ten times more often than I did before and still incur less expenses. Other hobbies that were important for our family were hiking, camping, and backpacking. I knew the hobbies we valued most were ones that would not cost us much. We now live within a two-hour drive of over a dozen renowned provincial parks. We have explored and camped at many of these spots already within our first years retired.

One source of entertainment that I have luckily avoided entirely for most of my life is the lottery. This source of spending is staggering for the average Canadian and represents a large share of many people's entertainment expenses. Just in Ontario, lottery sales amounted to $4.2 billion in 2019[21]. According to the Ontario Lottery and Gaming Corporation (OLG), 42% of Ontario adults or 5.1 million people are lottery players[22]. This amounts to each lottery player spending $823 per year. The numbers in the other provinces are comparable and even higher in some regions. This could mean that an average lottery-playing couple is spending $1,600 in lottery per year. Many are probably topping the average.

$1,600 per year invested properly over the course of a thirty-year career would generate over $100,000 adjusted for inflation. Although lotteries can let you dream of an early retirement the reality is the odds of winning are astronomical. Worst of all, this hobby could actually be delaying your realistic dreams of retirement. An extra $100,000 of savings in your lifetime would absolutely mean an earlier retirement, even if only by a few years. So, it is worth examining this spending category very closely. If you find enjoyment in the game of lottery, then it may still be worth it. But as is the case with all your discretionary expenses, you should analyze them and make sure they reflect what you value or what you are aiming for.

Travel
We always loved to travel and knew that with so much free time, we would want to travel more, not less. Travelling with children obviously costs more, but there are solutions. For example, being able to travel any time of the year and able to take advantage of enormous flexibility when choosing a vacation. We could also travel slowly and spend an entire month somewhere since we wouldn't have jobs to come back to. In the first summer after we retired, we spent twenty-nine days exploring the East Coast of Canada.

Individually or by the week, each trip or vacation probably cost us less in retirement due to our options and flexibility. However, we planned to do more of these trips and for longer periods of time. So, we were realistically looking at spending double our current $4,000/year budget or even more. Again, we knew travelling would be a discretionary expense that could be trimmed anytime if things didn't work out. We also knew that we could increase this budget line dramatically any given year by deciding to generate additional work-related income for a few months in a year.

Internet + Cell Phones
Reliable and fast internet is always important. For this reason, we did not anticipate spending less

on this service in retirement. We always try to seek out the best and cheapest options that meets our needs. We were spending $60/month on high-speed internet with no long-term contract at the time. We would continue to evaluate internet providers once per year to see if there were better options. This is a definite best practice for any household when it comes to telecommunication services. Big companies like Rogers and Bell make most of their money on people who grow complacent and never shop around, only to realize five years later that they are paying over $200 on their combined cable/phone/internet bill.

We had cut the cord on cable television long before we embarked on our financial independence journey. We just never saw enough value in maintaining this service when everything we enjoyed watching was online. We continued to watch almost all our shows and movies on Netflix for $10/month.

We were paying $15/month as a family for our cell phone service. This would not change in retirement. You might be wondering how this was possible. We realized that other than when going to work, both adults would rarely be out of the house separately at the same time. For example, when one of us was at the grocery store, running errands or out with friends, the other was most likely at home with the kids. And whenever we were both out of the house, we were more than likely together. For this reason, we realized that we only really needed one phone. Whenever we were separated, the one who was home could communicate with the other via our iPads using our home internet. Going to just one cell phone might sound crazy to most and to us it did at first. But it was actually quite liberating when we did it. I really enjoyed not being tied to a cell phone all the time. On the days when Danielle has the family cell phone, I don't have to worry about anyone trying to reach me or any other kinds of distractions.

Realizing we can do all of our online activities while at home, we also have not had a data plan for five years. This has allowed us to take advantage of the ultra-low-cost talk and text phone plans available from many providers for $15/month.

We constantly shop around when it comes to cell phone plans and always avoid contracts. We have always obtained our devices on our own by buying them second hand on Kijiji or eBay. Our current phone is a Samsung Galaxy S6, which we bought used in 2017 for $200; it was still in the box because the person selling it didn't like it. At the time, this phone retailed for over $500 new. We are still using that same reliable phone, nearly four years later with no plans to upgrade it anytime soon.

Life Insurance
When we were expecting our first child we started to think more about our finances and ways to protect our children should the worst happen: "What if one or both of us died?" We bought life insurance and it was the right thing to do. When our life really started getting serious and we had a house and a child on the way we did much reading and analyzed our expenses and living situation. We came up with a value of required money if one or both of us died so that our children would be okay.

This number was $800,000. It assumed we would live in our crazy, super-expensive mansion forever. We had planned enough money to pay that mortgage off outright. We also planned to supplement the deceased spouse's income for ten years. After undergoing all the required medical tests and completing all the questionnaires, we had our policy which costs us $55 per month. In hindsight, $800,000 is insane but it was what was proposed to us from the financial world at the time. It would have been a great strategy if we were planning on living the same lifestyle and requiring 100% of our incomes. But we soon decided that we were going to live in a mortgage-free home and live on less than 30% of what our incomes actually were. We definitely needed life insurance back then but probably not that much. We would have likely still needed such insurance, had we not changed many things in our lives.

Once we reached financial independence, we wouldn't be relying on a "working income" so the need to supplement a lost income became obsolete. Also, if one of us did die, the family unit would shrink by one adult so the overall expenses of the household would naturally reduce substantially. Our passive income would be designed to still produce even with just one adult.

Another reason to have life insurance is in case both of us would die. We have accumulated a sizable net worth which would be passed on to the people we designated to be our children's guardians if we ever both passed. Additionally, as we will discuss in a later chapter, we have accumulated significant education savings (RESPs) so our children's education will never be a financial obstacle.

Once we cancelled our policy, we generated an additional $660 of savings per year.

Predictions vs. Reality

We have now been retired for three years. Our constant focus on analyzing our expenses allows us to see how accurate our predictions were and if our early retirement plans were in fact realistic. Our travel expenses have topped nearly $8,000 per year. We have spent at least thirty days each summer camping and exploring our country. We have gone on a Caribbean cruise and an all-inclusive vacation. Our three-year spending average also includes over $6,000 we had to forfeit on a Mediterranean cruise we had paid for in 2018 but had to cancel at the last minute due to complications in the pregnancy of our third child.

All our other spending was quite accurate and sometimes lower. Our diligent year-end analyses have revealed that we have not surpassed $30,000 in annual spending in any full year so far. This is very encouraging for two reasons. First, it has reinforced our confidence in our plan long term and it has made us realize that we truly did not have to sacrifice anything we enjoyed in our lives.

Second, when we started on our path to early retirement, we had just focused on the forecasts of the big three categories discussed in chapters five to seven (childcare, housing, and transportation). We had forecasted that we would need passive income of $30,000 to safely retire from our jobs. This forecast turned out to be accurate even with some higher spending in the discretionary categories. In the next section of the book, we will elaborate on the keys to saving and generating the passive income needed to retire. We based our needs on $30,000 per year of income but just as we did with our spending, we came to realize that we happily surpassed our expectations once again.

PART 3: SAVING

CHAPTER 10

Your Net Worth

The best way to measure how close you are to your retirement goals is by calculating your net worth. Your net worth is the value of everything you own, minus everything you owe. My six-year-old son owns a few hundred dollars of Legos and other toys, some clothes, and a bike. Everything he owns is worth about $2,000. Because the banks won't lend him any money, he has no debts. So, his net worth is approximately $2,000.

The average family has a house, one or multiple vehicles, some savings and pensions. They also typically have a mortgage, one or two car loans, and sometimes a line of credit or some credit card debt. To calculate your family's net worth, simply add up these two categories honestly. By honestly,

I mean, calculating these items not based on what they are worth to you but based on what they are actually worth in an open market today. You may really value your Ford F-150 pickup truck, but it's only worth what someone will pay for it. It's important to remember that you lose 10% of the value of a new vehicle as soon as you leave the dealership and nearly 20% by the end of your first year owning it.[23] Your $40,000 vehicle is probably worth closer to $30,000 if you owned it for a year.

You probably own other items such as furniture, however, unless you have a specific antique item that is worth an enormous value, it's advisable not to include these items in your net worth. Furniture is not something that generally retains its value and would probably represent a very low and likely incorrect percentage of your total net worth.

When it comes to your vehicles and your total savings, your net worth calculation is pretty simple. For your car, you simply take the market value of it today and deduct how much you owe on it. You will often see that with vehicles, they can actually contribute negatively to your net worth. In many cases, people owe more money on a vehicle than it is worth today. Sometimes the calculation will just reveal a break-even. Don't let that scare you from doing the exercise. For savings and investments that you hold, you can pretty accurately figure out what they are worth by looking at your most recent statements.

This exercise requires a little more planning when it comes to your house. To calculate an accurate valuation of your house, you can either hire a real estate agent or professional appraiser to get an idea of what it is worth based on the current market trends. Many real estate agents will offer you this service for free hoping to convince you to use their services if you decide to sell. You can also look at comparable houses for sale in your area yourself and see what they are priced at. Then you can deduct 5% or 10% of the averages you see to give yourself a conservative estimate of what the actual sale price of your home could be today. It's important to note that when you are aiming to calculate your net worth you want to come up with a realistic valuation and not a best-case scenario estimate. Once you've determined your house valuation, you can deduct what you owe on your mortgage plus the necessary expenses that arise out of selling (commission, legal etc.) and this will help you determine this part of your net worth. With the rising housing prices across Canada in the last few years, you may be surprised by how much of your net worth is tied to your primary residence.

It gets a little more complicated when it comes to

the most important line item in your net worth. I am talking about your pensions. This is the savings that most people overlook. People with employer-sponsored pension plans don't realize how lucky they are. An employer-sponsored plan, often referred to as a defined benefit plan, can add so much value to your net worth. When you work for an organization that provides a pension plan, you pay a certain percentage of your salary into the plan, and the organization matches it or sometimes even contributes more than you do. As of 2016, employer-sponsored pension plans in Canada were worth $1.7 trillion.[24] To put that figure in perspective, in 2016, that was more than double the Federal Government's public debt.[25] That just accounts for the 37% of Canadians that are covered by an employer-sponsored defined benefit plan.

Many other Canadians don't work for an organization that offers a defined benefit plan but that do offer to match employees' contributions to their own retirement fund (RRSPs). These are often referred to as defined contribution plans. As of 2020, 69% of Canadians have an RRSP account and the average value of RRSP accounts in Canada is $112,000.[26] All this data reveals that most Canadians might underestimate how much their pensions or retirement savings might add to their actual net worth.

On the surface, you may not see your pension plan as belonging to you because you think you have to wait until you are sixty or older to access it. However, these plans always have a value for you if you ever decide to leave your employer and leave the plan. There is always a payout amount, and that is what your plan is worth to you at any point in time. When you leave your employer, you normally have a choice to leave the money in the plan and receive a payout in the future based on your contributions and years of service. Or you can take a payout which is called the commuted value. The commuted value is the value that the fund would need to have to pay your future monthly payout. These values are most often calculated using current Government of Canada bond rates.

The Globe and Mail did a good analysis in 2020 on how today's historically low bond rates are leading many commuted values to be worth much more than historically expected.[27] They revealed that many Government of Canada long-term bonds are now paying less than 1%. Bond rates generally reflect the long-term safe expected rate of return on investments. When bond rates are very low, pension plans need to allocate more money to fund your future payout. So that is why a commuted value (your current value in the plan) is worth more today than during a period when bond yields may be much higher. During low interest rate periods, you can get a higher commuted value, however, it does mean that your payout may grow slower in the future if you are relying on similar bond investing as well.

When we quit our jobs in 2018, I had been taking advantage of my employer RRSP matching program during my eight-year career. As a result, I had amassed a value of $100,000. Danielle fared much better since she worked for the federal government and profited from a defined benefit plan. Most government or public sector jobs provide extremely generous defined benefit pension plans. Bond rates were just as low in 2018 and 2019 as they are today, so Danielle was able to secure a very good commuted value from her pension plan. She left eight years of service with a $200,000 payout. There are some restrictions on these payouts. We did have to keep most of the money in Registered Retirement Savings Plans (RRSP) with our financial institutions and have a large portion of that amount in Locked in Retirement Accounts (LIRAs). LIRAs operate similar to RRSPs in the sense that you have control over how it is invested. However, you generally can't withdraw the money until you reach the age of fifty-five. This was not a concern for us since we do not plan to use this money any time soon. I will discuss why we really like these RRSP and LIRA accounts and how we use them to our advantage in chapter fourteen.

Our employer pensions were a very effective forced savings account for us. We walked away from eight-year careers with sizable retirement funds. Our retirement savings alone, if invested properly, will grow to be more than enough for us to live on down the road. When we retired, our retirement savings represented almost a third of our total net worth. Because of great investment returns in the last few years, these accounts are on track to be worth almost $500,000 within the next five years.

Once you do your own exercise and determine what your net worth is, you will have a better understanding of how close or how far retirement could be for you. Even if this exercise reveals a very low or negative net worth it will still give you an accurate reflection of where you are. When we first calculated our net worth shortly after we got our first jobs and started paying off our student loans, we were looking at a -$30,000 net worth. Yes, we were in the dreaded negative ourselves. This was in 2010, just eight short years before we quit our jobs for good.

I still periodically calculate my family's net worth to make sure we are on the right track. We have been extremely lucky in the first few years of retirement and have seen our net worth continue to grow significantly, even without full-time career income. In the next few chapters, I will share the investment strategies that helped us reach a net worth of over $1 million today. These strategies allow us to continue to grow our assets and keep most of it while paying very little taxes.

CHAPTER 11

The Power of Compound Interest

In this chapter, I would like to dive into a simple but fascinating concept. I am a well-educated adult in business but I still get stumped occasionally by how powerful compound interest actually is. Wikipedia (or a Wikipedia contributor) provides a great definition of compound interest. It is the addition of interest to the principal sum of a loan or deposit, or in other words, interest on interest.[28] In my opinion, compound interest is so important and so overlooked when it comes to making financial decisions.

Albert Einstein once described compound interest as the eighth wonder of the world when he explained "he who understands it, earns it; he who doesn't, pays it." He said this long before society adopted our current consumer addiction to debt. You can judge the ethical dilemmas surrounding the concept of compound interest; however, for as long as there are incentives to earn money in the world, there will always be compound interest. I always take compound interest into account when making financial decisions. There are many financial calculators on the internet to help you out. One I found very useful is www.mustachecalc.com. Using this website's "Savings From Not Spending" calculator you can figure out how compound interest can drastically alter your financial future.

Think about that daily cup of coffee at Starbucks costing $2. If you made your own coffee at home for $0.10 instead, and invested the saved $1.90 over your thirty-year career with a reasonable inflation-adjusted 4% return, you would end up with an extra $40,000 in your bank account in 2021 dollars. That is almost enough money to buy a brand-new Tesla or to take a hundred-day world cruise. What if you decided to go down to one vehicle and eliminated your household's second $500/month car payment? Adjusted for inflation you could end up with an extra $180,000 in twenty years. Likely enough to allow you to retire a few years earlier.

The other day I was trying to devise an experiment to teach my son the value of saving money, and I was once again shocked by the hidden power of compound interest. He has a bank account with a local institution, however with such low interest rates, it's impossible for him to actually see his money grow. If I can't get him to physically see it grow, he won't properly understand the value of saving long term. Mr. Money Mustache's concept of the "bank of dad" inspired me to mimic his strategy with a more aggressive approach.[29] This strategy involves me (the parent) being the bank. My son will give me whatever money he wants to save in his bank, and I will update a spreadsheet or a bank book that shows his money growing. I invest his money into our long-term account, which will generate much higher returns. I can then pay him more than his student high-interest savings account rate of 0.01% annually. Using this strategy, you obviously have to assume a bit of costs since you will likely pay your child more interest, risk free, than you may earn. But it's a small cost considering they don't have that much money to save to begin with and considering it will teach them valuable financial lessons.

I wanted my son to clearly see his money growing. At six years old, that is difficult. So, I settled on 10% per week. This will sound like a crazy figure since it works out to nearly a 500% annual return on investment. But I wanted him to profit by at least $1 if he saved his $10 bill one week to the next rather than go buy a cheap toy at Dollarama. This would be a great exercise in teaching delayed gratification as well. But then I ran the numbers, and I quickly changed my mind since the power of compound interest is just too strong.

Let me explain by examining a potential scenario where my son decided to never spend his $10 for a full year. Additionally, he would also invest in the "bank of dad" an average of $3 every week which he earned doing his chores or that he received as gifts. At the end of a fifty-two-week period, I would owe him $5,600. At the end of two years or 104 weeks, I would owe our eight-year-old son just over $800,000. We would be bankrupt. This is obviously a comical but accurate calculation (run the numbers yourself). But it does show that compound interest is a lot more powerful than we may sometimes originally think. I ended up settling on a 5% weekly rate, in anticipation that he would eventually succumb to buying a Lego set after a few months of savings rather than financially ruin the family.

On the other side of the coin, it is very important to be wary of compound interest on any loan you have. The payday loan industry offers an extreme example of how one could suffer from the powerful effects of this concept. Some payday loan operators charge as much as $17 for a $100 loan for a fourteen-day period. This amounts to an annualized rate of 442%.[30] This is in line with the rate I had proposed paying my son. If someone got a $100 payday loan today with a fee of $17 every fourteen days which compounded, they would end up paying over $6,000 in interest by the end of a single year. Payday loans are quickly growing in popularity. According to one study by the Government of Canada in 2017, two million Canadians use payday loans each year.[31] No wonder we seem to see more and more of these types of storefronts popping up in major cities.

Credit card debts are not as bad as the predatory payday loans in our society, but they still pose a significant cost to anyone who has them. A 2017 study by TransUnion showed that the average Canadian carried $4,094 of credit card debt.[32] The average credit card interest rates are around 19%. In one scenario calculated by ratehub.ca, if you had a $5,000 credit card balance and just made the minimum payments, it would take you over twenty years to pay it off. In this scenario you would end up paying more than the original balance ($5,983 in total) in interest alone.[33] Essentially the cost of using a credit card for $5,000 in purchases would actually cost $11,000. That's like paying a 120% tax on that new sofa.

It's important to truly understand the power of

compound interest when you plan for your future. Interest paid over one month or one year sometimes feels insignificant. However, over a lifetime, it amounts to enormous sums. Interest earned, on the other hand, can have an equally but positive effect. The following chapters will illustrate how this power propelled us to early retirement.

CHAPTER 12

*Passive Income with
Real Estate*

When growing our net worth, we had to invest wisely. We also had to invest focused on generating enough cash flow to sustain our living expenses. In this chapter, I will share how we came to generate all the income needed for us to retire early. The most important investment in our retirement plan was real estate. I had studied real estate investing for many years and had closely observed a number of small-town markets to see where our limited financial assets could go the furthest.

In big cities like Ottawa and Toronto, multi-unit income properties are very hard to come by for under $1 million. However, in many small towns, you can find some for a fraction of the price with actual rents that are not that far off the big-city numbers. We had roots in Northern Ontario, so we had an idea of which towns could present good long-term investments. Many small towns in Canada are contracting in size and very little money is put into infrastructure. Some of these towns were at one time reliant on a certain resource or industry that has run out, became obsolete, or left town. So, although the real estate prices are very low, the long-term prospects are sometimes not very good.

On the other hand, some small towns are still growing, long after their main economic industry changed. Those towns that have maintained a strong economy, and economic services end up benefiting from a growth in population. That is because residents in neighbouring smaller towns will eventually flock to the slightly larger community when they start to lose vital stores and services such as groceries and churches.

The town we chose to buy our retirement home in provided plenty of positive income property opportunities as well. Sturgeon Falls is the main centre of the municipality of West Nipissing, about 30km north of North Bay, and less than 400km from Toronto.

Historically, Sturgeon Falls was a logging and pulp and paper town. When the mill closed almost twenty years ago, the town's economy suffered. But it has thrived and has even grown in population in every census since. It is a popular low-cost alternative to those who want to live close to the lake but work in the bigger nearby cities like North Bay and Sudbury (both less than one-hour drive away). It also has a growing retired population. Seniors from surrounding small towns often move here to be closer to the hospital once they sell their houses and look to move into apartment units.

We quickly noticed that demand for rental units was high and that a properly renovated and managed property could fetch very good tenants. We purchased our first rental property near the beginning of our journey to early retirement. We found a run-down four-plex that required significant work. This building was currently renting all four units for just under $3,000 per month. We knew right away that we could drastically increase this amount based on the demand in this town. The best part was the price. After long negotiations, we paid $180,000. We invested $40,000 as a down payment to make our first income property purchase.

In between our purchase and our closing date, two of the four units in this building became vacant, giving us a great opportunity to start our revitalization project. We started travelling almost every weekend to work on the property. We also hired my father and other local contractors to take on most of the higher-skilled work. The work was mainly cosmetic and also involved lots of cleaning. So, we did not have to spend a fortune. Within a year, our first two newly renovated units were rented; the other two apartments became empty shortly after.

When we were done with this project, we had spent $40,000 on top of the $40,000 we had invested as our down payment. We had also reduced the energy costs across the units by installing new energy-efficient hot water tanks, refrigerators, stoves, and heating appliances in every apartment. And we changed over half the windows. Within eighteen months, we found four great tenants. The revenue stream of this investment increased by $1,000 per month which represented a 33% increase (from $3,000 to $4,000 per month). Additionally, we were able to reduce the utility expenses by $250 per month. Our mortgage payment was still just under $700 per month.

With all the major repairs done, I knew we

wouldn't have any major unexpected expenses coming up. However, I also knew that we still needed to budget for approximately 1-2% of the building value annually for long-term maintenance such as the roof. But, with all things considered and setting aside a fair amount for long-term repairs, this property started to generate a cash flow of approximately $18,000 per year without considering the mortgage paydown. The mortgage paydown generated an additional $6,000 per year to our net worth. Our total investment of $80,000 resulted in an approximate 30% annual return on our investment. At the time of writing this book, this property is now valued at nearly $400,000. That represents more than double the original purchase price and has drastically increased our net worth.

We hit a home run on this property. With just this property, we generated the first $18,000 of the $30,000 we needed for our retirement life. We were now motivated real estate investors, patiently looking for our next diamond in the rough.

Our second major investment was very similar. After we were done with our first property, we found a triplex that was being sold by a creditor and had been on the market for over six months. The biggest problem with this property was not so much the work needed, but the environment inside the building. It was located on a good street downtown. Unfortunately, the existing tenants were a big problem, deterring almost every other investor. We knew this when viewing the units. The building had so much potential with three huge apartments with twelve-foot ceilings. Once upon a time this was a beautiful building that had been left to wither with no maintenance for at least a decade. The entire front facade was falling apart which gave the building infamous recognition across town as "that building".

The biggest unit had four bedrooms and was being operated as a rooming house. There was more garbage than furniture in the apartment with mattresses scattered across each room. The heating system had broken months earlier and because of a dispute with the landlord it had not been fixed. As a result, the occupiers relied on their oven as their primary source of heat. When we came in for an inspection, it was set at 400 degrees with the door left open. They actually described this to me like it was a normal thing to do. Every unit had multiple pets and all the tenants had serious complaints and issues with each other, resulting in weekly arguments and disputes.

We took a risk and dived in. Priced similarly to our first investment property, we paid $190,000 for this one. Per unit, the price was higher, but because of the size and location, the rents would be higher as well. This project required less work long term, however, we knew that in the short term there would be trouble.

We ran the numbers based on the price we could get it for, and we knew the cash flow would be more than enough to sustain the building even with no changes. With the assumption that everyone kept paying. So, we acquired it and started managing the tenants as best we could. We did not force anyone to leave as long as rents were paid. We did the required safety work including fixing handrails, addressing the heating sources in every unit and other pressing maintenance issues. We installed new siding on the front of the building, which gave it a brand-new look. The building started regaining a positive reputation in town. But we did not invest any more than we had to.

We got our headaches in the first year. Disputes between the tenants often led to police presence. The tenants constantly had arguments over debts or drugs. They would try to convince us to kick out the other by claiming that they dealt them drugs. The accused just said that it was the other way around. I would advise them to discuss these criminal accusations with actual police.

One time in early spring, we were called by a special investigator who needed access to the property's shed right away. I rushed over to meet with officers of the municipal police. They informed me that someone tipped them off that there may be a dead dog in the shed. When we entered the shed, there were swarms of flies everywhere. The tip was a good one. There was indeed a dead dog in our shed. The investigation would later reveal that one of the tenants was simply waiting for the ground to thaw so they could go bury the dog they lost over the winter. When the other tenant discovered what was causing such a strong smell in their shared storage space, they called the authorities.

On another occasion, when the tenants fell behind on paying their rent, they assured me they had secured the funds to pay me within twenty-four hours, but I just needed to meet them to sign a document. I discovered that the document in question was listing me as a guarantor on a payday loan with a 500% annual interest rate. They did not understand my refusal to accept getting paid with a preposterously high-interest loan. One that I would be ultimately responsible for.

Eventually we got lucky and the tenants' hatred for each other led to the vacancy of two units. We had about twelve truckloads of leftover furniture, mattresses, and garbage to haul away. The last tenant with four cats stayed throughout all this but vacated shortly thereafter, which allowed us to turn over all three apartments in the same year.

We went to work applying all the same techniques we used on our first income property. Within a few months we again had a fully rented triplex with much better residents. Rents were now 20% higher than before and utility expenses had been reduced. Largely because the primary heating method was no longer a cooking stove.

The renovations to this property only required us to add $20,000 in addition to our down payment. We were again accounting for 1-2% of the building's value towards maintenance and repairs long term. Our second income property was now projecting an annual cash flow of at least $13,000 plus the mortgage paydown.

In just three years we invested less than $150,000 to produce an annual cash flow that had reached $31,000. This was more than enough to cover our projected living expenses.

Investing in real estate was the solution to grow our net worth and quickly increase our passive income. It wasn't easy. In the three years before our retirement, we spent countless days doing work nobody would ever choose to do. We scrubbed and cleaned toilets. We ripped out rotting and piss-stained carpets. We hauled almost one hundred loads of garbage to the landfills. We gave up lots of our downtime during this period, travelling most weekends in order to go work on our properties. In the end it was worth it.

Our scenario is not unique. So many people have gotten rich while investing in income properties. As opposed to the people on TV, we weren't trying to get rich by over leveraging our financial position. The get-rich-with-real-estate dream we sometimes hear about, involves owning dozens of properties with maxed-out mortgages on every one of them. It involves creating six-figure income streams. It could work, but there is no way owning a dozen or more income properties could be considered "passive". No matter how much you outsourced.

We also knew we didn't need a six-figure income. We just wanted to create a small passive income stream. We made sure to shield ourselves from a real estate collapse. We put a full 20% down payment on our properties and paid for all our renovations ourselves. This later resulted in having nearly 50% equity in both buildings. A very safe equity position to protect our investments long term.

Our location is not unique either. You don't have to move to our small Northern Ontario town to get the same results as us. We found a good real estate market with great potential to generate cash flow. There are hundreds of comparable markets and towns in Canada. You just need to do your research. You need to find a suitable low cost of living area where you would be comfortable settling down. A market with a relatively strong demand for renting and good prospects for the future. Any property can generate modest cash flows. In order to bring those cash flows into overdrive, you have to find a property that's in distress and far from its potential. And then work hard... That's the simple formula.

Some people thought that the cash flow of just two income properties could not possibly be enough to sustain our lifestyle. But we went on to push the envelope even further. We had much more free time in retirement, so we were able to increase our attention on our properties. Since being retired we have been able to add further efficiencies and upgrades to our buildings. As a result, our expenses continue to lower, and our rents continue to increase when vacancies occur. Two years into our retirement we ran our cash flow numbers again. We realized that we could now achieve our $30,000 cash flow goal with just one property instead of two if we just eliminated the mortgage on the better-performing one. Our numbers also indicated that we could eliminate the mortgage of one property with the proceeds of the other.

In 2020, the housing market in our small town was booming. This led to the realization that with some additional minor upgrades, we could sell one of our buildings for a pretty good profit. Even after only three years of ownership. Once we sold this property, we freed ourselves from all remaining mortgages or liabilities in our life.

Today, even when accounting for some ongoing maintenance and a contingency fund, we generate our $30,000 cash flow with just one single-income property.

The key to successful real estate ownership is similar to many lessons in life: do not get too comfortable. We have been lucky in acquiring good and reliable tenants. But in order to maintain our investments and cash flow, we make sure to not take our revenue streams for granted. We constantly think of ways to improve our property and take care of all important issues as soon as possible so we can compete for the best tenants on the market.

I knew that relying solely on rental income was a bit of a risk, so our plan had contingencies. In the next chapter I will elaborate on our non real-estate investment strategies that helped us further grow our net worth and diversify our assets.

CHAPTER 13

*Investing Outside
of Real Estate*

I didn't feel comfortable enough retiring if all we had was real estate investments. I knew we needed additional financial security beyond just a steady rental income stream. I was confident that most years our real estate income would sustain our entire lifestyle expenses and would even provide a surplus during some periods. But I also knew that just like any investor, we could see some bad years. Being quite a risk-averse person, I always think of the what-ifs. What if our real estate investments took a turn for the worse? What if we ran into a few bad tenants at the same time and were not getting paid our rents for months? Our plan needed to have contingencies built in.

I also had to think of a time in the future when we may no longer want real estate investments. A future when we would want to go from "somewhat passive" investments to "completely passive" investments.

We retired with a net worth of over $750,000 but we planned that this amount would only grow as we got older. At the time of writing this book, just three years into retirement, our net worth has already grown by almost 50% to $1.1 million. We anticipate doubling or tripling this value over time, just by making smart investment decisions. In this chapter, I will outline our investing plan outside of real estate. A large portion of our net worth continues to be outside of real estate, and one day, our financial investments will likely represent the majority of our assets.

As I described in the previous chapters, we left our eight-year careers with $300,000 in pension savings. We cashed out our employer pension plans and have complete control over these funds. All that money is in tax-sheltered accounts (more on this in chapter fourteen and we control how it is invested.

We will not be touching this money. Or rely on it at all. We continue to treat this as our traditional pension money. We have successfully lived on the cash flow of our real estate holdings for three years, so we know we can continue to let our pension money grow untouched. This was truly "what if" money. In the unlikely scenario that all else failed and we could no longer live on our real estate investments, then we would have to return to traditional jobs. If our real estate holdings did provide adequate cash flow for us to raise our family and live comfortably for the next twenty years but we lost it all later on, we still had pension savings.

On the surface, $300,000 does not sound like an enormous amount of money for two adults to rely on for a retirement. But I will elaborate on the investment strategy we follow which has historically grown at an average of at least 7% per year. When you account for a generous average annual inflation rate of 2%, you are left with a real growth of at least 5% per year. Between the ages of thirty and sixty, our $300,000 pension savings will likely grow to $1.3 million in 2020 dollars.

By the time we are sixty, we likely won't have any dependent children. So, our annual expenses will be lower. But even if we see a surge in our living expenses beyond inflation, we will still be fine relying only on our retirement savings. Using a more conservative $1 million value of this fund in thirty years, and a more conservative 3.5% withdrawal rate to live out in our golden years, we can see that we will always have a steady cash flow of at least $35,000 per year.

In addition to our pension savings, in the last ten years all our other surplus savings have been put into tax-free savings accounts. We have accumulated over $200,000 in these accounts and continue to add to them every year.

So how do we actually invest our $500,000 of liquid net worth? I'll explain how we confidently expect to achieve high long-term growth using pretty simple financial instruments.

Exchange Traded Funds
All our investment assets have always been in Exchange Traded Funds (ETFs). I will attempt to give you a brief introduction to ETFs and how we use them in our investment strategy.

ETFs are an investment fund that operates like a stock in the market. These funds can hold all sorts of assets in the form of stocks, commodities, and bonds. There are hundreds of ETFs traded on all the stock markets. They all have different goals. Most ETFs track a certain index. For example, tracking the Toronto Stock Exchange index or the New York Stock Exchange index. Tracking the index essentially means that the fund goes up or down with how the overall index does. An ETF tracking just the Canadian Stock Market (TSX) would go up 10% in a year that the TSX, as a whole, goes up 10%, and it would go down 10% in a year that the market goes down 10%.

ETFs could also track the price of valuable metals like gold and silver. Or one could just focus on tracking the hundred largest oil-related companies in the world. In that case, the fund would hold proportional shares in a hundred other stocks, and its value would go up or down with how the whole oil sector performed.

Other ETFs strictly hold bonds in Canada or in the rest of the world. Bonds are financial instruments issued by corporations and governments to fund their operations. A bond is essentially like a loan. When you buy a Canadian government bond, you are lending the government money at a set interest rate, which they pay you annually (ex. 1% every twelve months). Bonds are considered much safer than stocks because they have a set interest rate and are pretty much guaranteed to be paid back (unless the corporation or government goes bankrupt). Bond market ETFs are funds that track all the bonds available in a certain market or industry. For example, an ETF may seek to own a piece of every corporate or government bond (or both) issued on the Canadian market.

ETFs are similar to the traditional long-term savings instrument of choice: mutual funds, with some key differences. With a mutual fund, there is a company or individual that picks and chooses which stocks to invest in, month-to-month or year-to-year in that fund. Some mutual funds do better than others. They could have better-than-average years followed by below-average years. In contrast, ETFs are typically automated with no picking of stocks involved. Two ETFs offered by different companies following the same index should perform the same year-to-year. Mutual funds will typically hold many classes of assets in one fund while many ETFs will hold just one type (i.e. just stocks, or just bonds).

The most important difference between these two types of investment funds are fees. Mutual funds operate by claiming to intelligently pick the best stocks for their portfolio on any given year. For this reason, they have a higher management expense ratio (MER). The MER of a fund is the total cost you pay to own that fund. It includes the costs to operate the account and the commission to the investment advisor among other things. These fees are usually between 0.5% to 2.5% of your investment in mutual funds. So, you pay the managers of the mutual fund up to 2.5% of your portfolio every single year, regardless of how the fund performs.

ETFs make no claim of intelligent picking, so the MER is drastically less, with most costing less than 0.30% and some as low as 0.10%. The differences in fractions of percentages do not seem like much but it can add up to hundreds of thousands of dollars long-term. On a one-million-dollar portfolio, a 2% difference in fees will add up to $218,000 in just ten years when compounded. When accounting that the lost money could have been invested, the shortfall is almost $300,000. So, management fees definitely do matter. To put it another way, on a $1 million mutual fund with a 2% management fee, you are paying someone $20,000 per year to manage that money. With the same amount in an ETF with a 0.2% management fee, you are only paying $2,000 per year.

In a traditional ETF portfolio, you do however incur additional minor costs when you buy and sell the funds you are in. This would happen when you want to initially invest or when you want to add money to your account. If you have a portfolio of multiple ETFs it is advisable to rebalance the portions in each ETF once per year to make sure you are maintaining your desired split. In order to do this, you have to sell some shares of one or more ETFs and then buy shares of another.

Typically, these transactions range from costing as much as $10 to being free with some online brokerages. The most trades I have ever made in a single year was ten, which cost me less than $100.

With ETFs, there is no single person or company that picks and chooses stocks. The funds strictly track a market or industry. If the goal of the fund is to track the entire Canadian stock market (the TSX) then the fund will hold a proportional amount of every single company listed on the TSX. And it will rebalance these holdings regularly so that the fund is always holding a virtual slice of the entire market. Most of the trading and tracking is not done by humans but by computers and algorithms.

You might wonder if there is value in someone picking stocks rather than it being a robot. For some people, there is value in choosing mutual funds. Sometimes mutual funds offer more services like automatic monthly contributions, monthly reports, and more hand holding in general for the everyday investor. With ETFs, you are more on your own, and take a more hands-on approach to your portfolio. I for one have felt more comfortable with robots handling our money than people and here's why.

I tend to agree with many experts that think

that stocks on the markets are generally always perfectly priced. The stock market could be described as an example of perfect market competition. Perfect market competition is an economic theory that characterizes a market where it is almost impossible to make a profit long term by strictly buying and selling. A perfect market always prices commodities perfectly so there is no room to buy something lower and sell it higher.[34] An example of this would be a farmers market. At a farmers market, many vendors are selling the same products. Because they know the buyers are going to browse around and see the differences in prices, most of the similar goods are priced the same.

There are so many people buying and selling stocks every day across the world. They quickly buy when they perceive a stock to be too low and sell when they perceive it to be too high. Because of this, gaps between the price of an asset and what it is worth, rarely happen. You can't say that the Apple stock or the Google stock is worth more than what the stock market says. Because the million buyers in the market have already learned every piece of information about Apple and Google and bought and sold on that information. So, the price is as accurate as possible.

For these reasons many economists argue that

stock markets are a perfect market. A stock broker could claim to do better than the rest of the market in any given year or over a few years. However, for every broker that claims to achieve better results than the market "average" there has to be another broker who lags the average. And when it comes to investments, you should always be looking past just a few years. Especially if you are retiring early. You need your investments to grow for forty or fifty years or more. A stock broker or financial fund who claims to beat the average can never continue to beat it forever. Every fund, company, or even superstar have bad years or sometimes have their luck change course drastically. Warren Buffet, highly regarded as the world's best stock picker, has even had years where he did worse than the "average". Warren Buffett himself will even claim that most people should not be in the business of picking their own stocks. He has often said throughout the years that everyone should stick to index funds.[35]

Jack Bogle famously said "Don't look for the needle in the haystack. Just buy the haystack" to emphasize the value of picking a market rather trying to beat that market. Jack Bogle was the founder and longtime leader of Vanguard, one of the largest investment firms in the world with over $6.2 trillion in assets under management.[36] Vanguard is credited with creating the first ever

Exchange Traded Fund. He rightly claimed that you are always better off buying the whole haystack rather than trying to find (or hiring someone to try and find) the needle in that proverbial haystack.

Couch Potato Investing

So which ETFs do we invest in? There are many ETF providers on the market today, offering all sorts of funds that follow one market or another. We follow a variation of the "Canadian Couch Potato" investing model popularized by Dan Bortolotti from MoneySense magazine. This investment strategy emphasizes the use of a few ETFs investing in three broad categories.[37]

1. The Canadian Stock Market
2. The U.S./International Stock Markets
3. The Canadian and International Bond Markets

The Couch Potato model can be used with different percentages allocated to each category depending on your risk acceptance and long-term investing plans. With a conservative approach you would be taking much less risk but with less potential for long-term gains. For this approach, you would focus a larger portion of your money in the bond market.

One example of a conservative "couch potato"

model would allocate approximately 70% of your funds to bond markets. The other 30% would be allocated to Canadian and International stocks.

Under a more balanced approach, the split would be 50% stocks or equities and 50% in bonds. And if you were investing with an aggressive or growth strategy, you would allocate about 80% to stocks or equities and only 20% to bonds. You can change all the ratios based on your preferred risk level. The amount you invest in stocks or equities should also be diversified with a certain amount invested in the Canadian market and some invested in the U.S./International markets depending on your risk appetite.

Once you establish what your investment strategy is, and you purchase your ETFs based on your desired split, you need to rebalance it annually to make sure your desired split stays the same. This is because in any given year, the bond market or the stock market can do better or worse, which will skew the overall numbers. This will cause your allocation split to be different than what you intended.

We are investing with a very long-term goal. We don't plan to use our invested money anytime soon, so we are investing with a twenty or thirty-year horizon. Because of this, we have always invested pretty aggressively. With an aggressive or growth strategy you are bound to have some really bad years when the market crashes such as in 2008 or even in early 2020, since you have the majority of your holdings in stocks. However, the data is pretty clear that in the long term you come out way ahead. Historical trends show that a well-placed growth portfolio will generate average annual returns of over 7% even when accounting for the occasional crashes.

The difference in growth between a conservative and aggressive portfolio is sometimes 2% or more annualized long term. This may not seem like much (when you compare an annual growth of 5% to 7%) however if you compound this over twenty-five years, the difference is enormous. If you invested $500,000 over twenty-five years using an investment strategy that generated 5% growth per year, you would end up with $1.7 million at the end. This is a pretty good amount but is dwarfed when you compare it to a strategy that would generate 7% annual growth. A $500,000 portfolio invested over twenty-five years generating 7% growth would yield $2.7 million. The difference between these two scenarios is a staggering $1 million.

Before deciding that ETFs are the right investment platform for you, I would suggest you do further reading on the website www.canadiancouchpotato.com. On this website, you will find so much valuable information on the concept and strategies of ETF investing as well as model portfolios to follow based on your desired risk levels.

Another great resource to consult before starting your investing journey are investor questionnaires. Many financial planners will have you complete these types of questionnaires when you become their client, to determine your personal level of risk tolerance. These types of questionnaires can help you figure out what your investing goals are and determine if you are inclined to be a more conservative or aggressive investor. Today, you don't necessarily need to see a financial planner to take one. Vanguard Canada has one such questionnaire available directly on their website (just search Google for Vanguard Canada investor questionnaire). At the end of one of these questionnaires you are provided with a bit of a snapshot into your mind and get a better idea of your financial goals and risk appetite.

Asset Allocation ETFs
In recent years, some companies have started offering Asset Allocation ETFs. These are ETFs which are composed of ETFs. So, an ETF full of

ETFs... I know that sounds confusing, but these new instruments make smart and simple investing so much easier.

As I mentioned earlier, with our aggressive investment strategy we invest approximately 80% of our funds in equities and 20% in bonds. In the past we would purchase and hold a combination of four or five ETFs. This would include stock market ETFs with Canadian and U.S./International exposure with 80% of our money in addition to a bond ETF with the other 20%. We would then rebalance our ETFs once a year to make sure we maintained our desired split.

Recently, we have converted all our investments to the Growth Asset Allocation ETF managed by Vanguard. This ETF trades under the ticker VGRO on the Toronto Stock Exchange. This ETF holds seven other ETFs in its portfolio, representing a very well-diversified option. You can see the full breakdown of this ETF and what it is invested in on Vanguard Canada's website. It allocates 80% of the fund to stock ETFs which not only track the Canadian stock market (24% of the fund) and the U.S. stock market (33% of the fund) but also the world stock markets. It allocates 17% of the fund to the developed world stock markets (excluding Canada and the U.S.) and 6% to emerging market (or developing world) countries' stocks. Vanguard also offers more conservative versions of Asset Allocation ETFs. Although Vanguard was the first company to offer such a product, other institutions such as BMO and iShares now offer similar ETFs.

Asset Allocation ETFs do come with a slightly higher MER of approximately 0.25%. If you were to purchase your own ETFs outside of an Asset Allocation ETFs you would likely pay average MERs between 0.15% and 0.20% on your mix of ETFs. So, this type of fund costs a little more. However, you do save in transaction costs as you never have to rebalance the portfolio. With an Asset Allocation ETF, the fund itself continues to maintain the desired split by buying and selling the ETFs it follows periodically without you having to make trades.

To close this chapter, I would like to share three important tips to keep in mind when you start thinking about your investment strategy.

1. Keep an eye on the MER: It's important to not just look at the Management Fee of a mutual fund or ETF, but to also look at the Management Expense Ratio (MER). The management fee normally takes into account the costs to manage the fund but will leave out some legal and administrative costs. Some financial products still advertise management fees while the majority now mostly stick with the standard MER. The MER represents the total cost of holding an asset. When it comes to mutual funds, you will sometimes see a management fee of 1.5% but an overall MER of 2.5%. This is very misleading as your annual cost on a $100,000 asset is $2,500 and not $1,500 ($1,000 difference). For ETFs, the differences are not huge. For example, the ETF we closely follow, VGRO, has a management fee of 0.22% and an MER of 0.25%.

2. Use the right financial advisors: Most people will still benefit from speaking to financial advisors. I do think that many financial advisors have a conflict of interest when they promote mutual fund options, as they stand to receive significant commissions, rather than promoting an ETF index investment approach where they would not. There is a growing number of financial planners that are now offering "fee only" services. These advisors don't accept commissions and charge their clients a fee directly for their advice. This is what I would recommend for most people, and an option we would even entertain in the years to come in order to get a second look at our own investment strategies. If you have a retirement portfolio of $500,000 and are paying mutual fund fees of 2.5%, you are effectively paying $12,500 in fees per year. It would be worth an additional fee from a fee-only advisor if they could steer you to a portfolio that would cost even just 0.5% less (a savings of $2,500 per year).

3. Use the right accounts: The best reason to speak to a financial planner may not be solely to decide what type of investments you should be in, but to also decide what type of accounts your money should be in. The right investment plan must focus on what financial vehicles your money is invested in. I will discuss this in the next chapter when I outline the various tax-sheltered accounts available in Canada.

CHAPTER 14

Tax-Sheltered Accounts

Tax sheltering can sometimes be a controversial topic. Some people will automatically think of wealthy billionaires hiding their money in offshore bank accounts to avoid paying taxes in their home country. But there are legal and readily available ways to shelter your money in Canada. Sheltering your money for tax purposes is essentially a strategy to try to reduce your tax obligations to the government. The governments themselves promote many of these options as a way to incentivize people to save.

Tax-sheltered accounts can help you save and grow your money tax free. They can also reduce your reported income. Beyond just using tax-sheltered accounts, there are many ways to reduce your reported income at the end of the year. Reducing your reported income not only gives you financial benefits in the form of lower taxes, it can also positively affect you with much higher government benefits.

In this chapter, I will discuss the two main tax-sheltered accounts available in Canada: the Tax-Free Savings Account (TFSA) and the Registered Retirement Savings Plan (RRSP). I will explain the tax benefits of using these accounts and the effects they can have on one of the most important government benefits available to young families, the Canada Child Benefit (CCB). In examining their benefits, I will propose some examples where they can be extremely beneficial to early retirees like ourselves. At the time of writing this book, we have been able to keep the entire share of our non real estate net worth inside tax-sheltered accounts. This has led to us having an almost zero tax burden and gives us the potential to maximize our eligibility for government social benefits.

Tax-Free Savings Accounts (TFSA)
The Tax-Free Savings Account was launched by the Canadian government in 2009. It would prove to be one of the most useful tools for any young investor. When this idea was launched, it allowed every adult Canadian to invest up to $5,000 per

year into an account that would grow tax-free. This meant that whatever growth or profit your $5,000 gained, it would not be subject to taxes and would not be part of your taxable income. On the surface and at the beginning, this didn't seem like a substantial benefit for savers. But in the long term, the tax savings could be huge. Especially if you learn to live on a lower income. The annual $5,000 contribution has gone up throughout the years in $500 increments to reflect inflation.

As of 2021, the TFSA annual contribution limit is $6,000. The accumulated total at this point is $75,500 if you were at least eighteen years old in 2009. A couple today would have a combined limit of $151,000. If full contributions have been made since 2009, that amount could be worth much more. Today, we have over $200,000 in our TFSAs because of the tax-free growth.

If this program continues to exist for another ten years and we make the maximum allowable contributions, our accounts should accumulate an additional $300,000 and be worth over $500,000 in 2021 dollars. In just twenty years from now our combined accounts should be worth over $1 million, assuming similar historical stock market returns of the last twenty years (with three significant market downturns).

Why is maximizing your TFSA so important? Imagine yourself on your fiftieth or sixtieth birthday and you have a $500,000 or a $1 million (with your spouse) fund that is completely tax sheltered. You can now start drawing money from this account with no tax repercussions. Drawing 4% per year from $1 million can give a couple a $40,000 per year in tax-free income. Even if you decide to continue earning a bit of income part-time, as many early retirees do, you can still avoid almost all taxes. You could earn an additional $13,000 per year nearly tax-free (this is the basic personal amount that individuals can earn before paying taxes in Canada).

If this $1 million was outside of a TFSA and instead in an RRSP, or you were receiving $40,000 from a pension fund, then you would have to pay taxes on the income and report it as earned income from the first dollar. If you withdraw 4% per year, or if you earned a similar amount with a pension, then you would start with a reported income of $20,000 each, before you earned any other income. Here is how much the tax burden would be on the two scenarios described above in Ontario:

Scenario 1: A couple each withdrawing $20,000 per year from a TFSA and earning $13,000 each in part-time income.

Total taxes paid: $1,562 (this is because there is a small portion of provincial taxes on the earned income as well as a small percentage of CPP/EI premiums to pay).

Net income: $64,438

Scenario 2: A couple withdrawing $20,000 each from an RRSP and earning $13,000 each in part-time income.

Total taxes paid: $11,712

Net income: $54,288

The difference between these two scenarios is a staggering $10,150. This difference becomes even more pronounced if the sources of income outside the TFSA grows even more. This is not to say that the TFSA is where everyone should put their savings. But this example illustrates how powerful a tax-free savings account can be in the long term. Especially for those, like us, who can reduce their required retirement income. Or for those who would prefer not to necessarily retire in their forties or fifties but who would like to just work part-time.

Registered Retirement Savings Plan (RRSP)
RRSPs should also be taken very seriously when planning for retirement. Even more so when you are thinking of early retirement. RRSPs are an-

other investment account created by the Government of Canada to help people save. RRSPs are essentially a tax deferral account which is designed to help people save specifically for retirement. When you put money into an RRSP, you reduce your earned income in the year you contribute but will pay income taxes when you decide to take that money out. The growth of the money in the RRSP is not taxed either until you decide to take it out. Every Canadian can contribute 18% of their prior year's earned income (up to a maximum of $27,830 for 2021) minus any company-sponsored pension plan contribution.

I will try to describe the benefits of this type of savings plan with a super simplistic example. Imagine you have an income of $100,000 and are going to pay $27,133 in total taxes this year, including CPP/EI contributions (calculated using simpletax.ca). Now if you decide to put $15,000 in your RRSP this year, your tax bill goes down to $21,793 because you have a much lower earned income. As a result, you save $5,340 in taxes.

Now imagine the following year, you have now retired and don't have a working income. If you decide to take out the $15,000 from your RRSP you will only pay $1,011 in taxes on the withdrawal. You will have quickly realized a net tax savings of $4,329 for having used your RRSP for just one year.

The reason that this example is overly simplistic is that most people won't just make RRSP contributions for one year and then retire. But it illustrates the true benefits of an RRSP account: the deferral of income during years when you have high incomes to years when you have a much lower income. Such as in an extremely early, low-cost retirement. In certain cases however, some people will find themselves in higher tax brackets once they retire. In those cases, the benefits of a long-term RRSP are debatable. If you earn $40,000 at the beginning of your career, the deferral of taxes may not be offset in the future if you retire at sixty years old with a huge net worth and an overall retirement income of over $100,000. In this case, you may pay more taxes on your RRSP withdrawals at sixty, than what you saved back in your twenties. Nevertheless, this would still be a good problem to have.

Back to the potential benefits of using an RRSP. As I described earlier, you can earn approximately $13,000 as an individual each year in Canada while avoiding almost all taxes. This $13,000 can also come in the form of RRSP withdrawals. With that in mind, you could set yourself up with a plan that would generate $40,000 per year using a mix of an RRSP and a TFSA while paying virtually no taxes. The main benefit of such a strategy would be the tax savings during your working career while making RRSP contributions. Another benefit that we mostly enjoyed is that by using both RRSPs and TFSAs you can accumulate a very high net worth faster. This could allow you to accumulate enough assets to retire after a relatively short career.

An RRSP/TFSA hybrid plan could see a couple having combined RRSPs of $650,000 and combined TFSAs worth $350,000. Drawing down 4% of each account would result in $40,000 in income while paying zero taxes. If a couple with $70,000 salaries started maximizing their RRSP and TFSA contributions from scratch today with no assets, they could reach the numbers above in under fifteen years. So, it's never too late.

As I mentioned earlier, we have been able to maximize the use of these two accounts and have had to pay very little taxes in retirement. As of 2021, we are able to keep over $200,000 in TFSAs and $300,000 in RRSPs. While we continue on our current trajectory of relying on our real estate cash flow and allowing our other investments to grow, we will continue to accumulate additional room in our tax-sheltered accounts.

We are each allowed to add an additional $6,000 to our TFSAs each year. Additionally, we also accumulate 18% of our reported income every year in RRSPs contribution limits.

If we were to let these increased limits go unfulfilled for ten years, we would be faced with a great opportunity. In the future, we could decide to sell our remaining rental property and put all the proceeds in tax-sheltered accounts. While reducing our long-term financial risk, we will likely be able to convert our entire net worth into tax-sheltered accounts within the next decade. That is assuming we don't continue to find other ways to make money and grow our net worth even further.

Canada Child Benefit
The Canada Child Benefit (CCB) is not a tax-sheltered account. As I described earlier, it is a tax-free monthly payment given to Canadian parents to help with the cost of raising children. In chapter five I discussed how we could stand to benefit from up to $24,000 in a combination of the federal and provincial child benefits just by keeping our annual incomes under $30,000. We are a pretty extreme example, having three young children and significantly lower than average spending. But everyone should keep in mind the CCB when contemplating an early retirement with children.

You can easily explore different scenarios using

the CCB calculating tool offered by the Government of Canada[38]. A married couple earning and living off of $40,000 per year with two school-aged children living in Ontario, would receive nearly $14,000 per year. The same couple earning a combined $50,000 would receive $10,000 annually.

As I discussed in chapter five, we have avoided relying on these types of payments as a dependable income source in our retirement plan and you should as well. Governments and policies can change and drastically alter these types of programs so we cannot rely on them as a long-term income source to retire on. However, they are a significant benefit to offset the additional costs that come with incorporating children into your non-traditional retirement plans.

The CCB makes tax planning so important when exploring early retirement. That is why we always get our taxes prepared by a professional accountant that specializes in personal taxation. Even though Danielle herself is a CPA and I have an MBA, we do not live and breathe the tax code and are not experts in the field. The minimal costs of getting a professional to file our taxes can sometimes mean thousands in tax savings or CCB benefits.

CHAPTER 15

Investing for Your Children's Education

Having children affects many people's financial plans in their lives. When considering your early retirement options, you will undoubtedly think of the implications of doing so with children. As I touched on in prior chapters, there are many financial benefits available that offset the additional cost of raising children in a non-traditional retirement lifestyle. One cost that many parents think about is post-secondary education. I often hear how a university or college education is becoming so expensive and kids have to assume so much debt just to get enough education for a decent job.

Danielle and I both got through university assuming our financial costs and came out into the workforce with some debt. It was not crippling since we had worked as much as we could during university. We faced comparable tuition costs as kids do today. We paid approximately $5,000 a year in the last year of our undergraduate program ten years ago. According to a CBC Analysis in 2019 the average Ontario university tuition is $6,160 and the average college tuition is $2,768.[39] According to Statistics Canada, Ontario is very close to the Canada-wide average.[40] When adjusting for inflation, we were probably in the same boat as children are today. And with advances in technology and more social pressure for free post-secondary education across our society, I can't imagine that tuition costs will outpace inflation anytime soon. If anything, I believe they could start decreasing.

Although we got through our four-year undergraduate programs as well as through graduate and accounting certification programs (CPA for Danielle, MBA for myself) on our own financially, if we can provide some financial assistance to our kids at no costs to ourselves we will take advantage of it. In this chapter I will explain how you can also save a large amount for your children's education without sacrificing any of your own funds in the long term. I will show you how the Canadian government gives you the tools to pay for a four-year undergraduate degree or three-year diploma program for free. Using our strategy to save for your children's post-secondary studies, you can also benefit from a forced-savings plan that can help you achieve retirement much sooner.

What is an RESP?
A Registered Education Savings Plan (RESP) is an investment account available to Canadian parents (or other relatives or friends of a child). The government contributes 20% or $500 per year of the first $2,500 contributed by the account holder. For example, you contribute $2,500 per year and the government will provide a grant of $500 each year. The total lifetime grant contribution by the government is $7,200.

There are many ways to manage an RESP account through your bank or financial institution. There are also some financial companies that specialize exclusively in group RESP programs and they will try to entice parents to join them at baby or parent trade shows. I would advise against these companies as they generally operate the RESPs differently than a bank would and they seem to charge higher management fees. They may also offer less flexibility. To keep it simple just open your account with whatever bank you do most of your business with.

Once your money as well as the government grants are in an RESP you can manage it in many different ways. You can keep it in a high-interest savings account, but high-interest saving rates are pathetically low right now. You can invest it in a variety of mutual funds depending on your risk preference. My preferred choice is using an Asset Allocation ETF as I described in chapter thirteen Regardless of the option you choose, you should just aim for long-term growth as this is money that you are investing for eighteen years or more. This means that you shouldn't use it to buy and sell individual stocks short term just because you got a good tip.

Now that we got the basics of what an RESP account is and how you can open one and manage it, I will move on to how to give your child a free education following three easy steps.

Step 1: Maximize the grants and the growth
If you contribute $2,500 per year into an RRSP for fifteen years (in the fifteenth year, you only need to contribute half), then you will take full advantage of the $7,200 grants from the government. If your contributions and the grants are properly invested (even conservatively) they can grow substantially over the course of the child's life.

If you look at some of the target education mutual funds from the major banks, they generate average returns of almost 6% per year over the last five years. Although these are mutual funds, they do present easy-to-manage options for those wanting a simple option. Target education funds are designed to be a little bit more aggressive in the early years and more conservative in the years closer to when the money is needed. If you started an RESP today for a baby, you would likely opt for a Target 2035 or Target 2040 fund. Assuming you were invested in a fund like this with similar returns, you may expect an average of 5% return over an eighteen-year period. At the end of eighteen years, your $2,500 annual contributions (for 14.5 years) plus the government grants will have grown to: $80,144*.

To come up with this number I used a future value calculator. I calculated the future value of annual contributions of $3,000 for 14.5 years at 5% interest. And then took that amount and calculated the future value of 3.5 additional years with no annual contributions but still at 5% growth.

Step 2: Pay for your child's education

Now you take the $80,144 in this account and subtract the $36,250 you contributed yourself ($2,500 X 14.5 years). This will leave $43,894 to use to cover all your child's educational expenses.

Now you're probably thinking that $43,894 won't

be worth the same in eighteen years. So, we have to bring it back to 2021 dollars. After accounting for a safe 2% rate of inflation per year, the present value of this account at the end of eighteen years would be $30,690.

Today that $30,690 would cover an average four-year university degree in Ontario ($24,640) with money left over for books and incidentals. On the college side, this amount could easily pay for a three-year program plus incidentals, books, and residency costs (if your child decides to study out of town).

Step 3: Pay yourself back
In this step you take your money back. As per the RESP rules, you can withdraw all the principal payments you made with no taxes or penalties. That is because those $2,500 contributions were made with after-tax dollars already, so they have already been taxed by the government. So, you are free to transfer your $36,250 share to your retirement savings via your TFSA or RRSP.

You can do this even before you decide to close the account but if you don't need the money right away, you could leave it in the RESP until your child is done with their schooling. In case you decide you want to help them further down the road. An RESP can stay open for thirty-five years.

By using just the grant and growth portion of the RESP account you could pay for your child's entire university or college education. I realize that there are other related expenses (such as housing and transportation) but just paying for their tuition will give your children a huge financial advantage starting their post-secondary education. Contrary to the common thinking these days, I don't think parents should feel obligated to pay for all of their children's post-secondary education. Teenagers and young adults can work during their summers or after school and save up. They are in fact going to study to get a job that will generate their future income so they should have a financial stake in it as well. I gained tremendous financial knowledge by being financially responsible for my entire post-secondary education. Being financially responsible is one of the best lessons you can teach your children and they won't learn it as well, if all their education and living expenses are paid for.

Withdrawing RESPs
To follow this strategy, you will have to withdraw from your RESP from the grant (government) portion or the growth portion of the RESP account and leave the principal balance in the account. These amounts are tracked separately. Grants can only be withdrawn for educational purposes (so if there are any left in the account when it is time to

close it, they are forfeited). The growth portion is taxed and can be penalized if you need to take it out under your name once the account is closed. But as I mentioned earlier, the principal balance can be withdrawn with no taxes or penalties. Consult with your financial institution when it comes time to withdraw funds.

In a scenario where you were planning to use all the money in the account for your child's education (i.e. no plan to withdraw back your principal) then you may need to be even more strategic in how you withdraw funds. Because the growth/grants portion of withdrawals will be taxed in your child's name, you may aim to reduce their tax burden and may use principal money in some years if they have other significant income (above the basic personal amount in your province).

Regardless of what you decide to do with your RESP it is important to have a withdrawal plan.

If your child doesn't go to school or does not need any of the RESP money (because of grants or scholarships), then you could still benefit from all the growth accumulated in the account. Although all the government grant portion has to be returned, up to $50,000 of the growth can be transferred to your RRSP account if you have room. If you anticipate this to be the case, make sure you build up some RRSP room if you don't already have some.

Remember that you can keep an RESP open for up to thirty-five years so you have plenty of time to plan how to close this account.

Final Thoughts on Education
When deciding how to plan for your child's education it's also important to consider the financial assistance options available. This is especially important if you decide to retire early. Many government grants for students are based on the parents' income. So, you may have one additional incentive to reduce your annual expenses and required annual income.

The OSAP (Ontario Student Assistance Program) has a calculator that estimates how much your child is eligible in grants and loans. Other provinces have similar calculators available as well. A quick estimate based on our current household income showed that if each of our children started a four-year university degree today, they would be eligible for $7,000 in grants (not loans) each year. I also tested the calculator using a hypothetical family with only two dependents and with a family income of $100,000 and the grant portion available from the government was still $2,000 per child. So, most households do benefit.

There are many financial options available for students today and there is a good chance that there will be more in the future. The post-secondary industry could also change drastically. Programs could become longer or shorter. Tuition could become entirely government funded. All these scenarios may mean that an RESP is not required in the future or even today.

PART 4: RETIRING

CHAPTER 16

Identity

In the last section of the book, I will share what retirement means to me. Specifically, how I have dealt with the identity of being retired young. Some people will suffer midlife crises near the midpoint of their life in their forties or fifties. A midlife crisis is typically associated with the realization that your mortality is closer or due to a sense of lack of accomplishment in your life. In my case, I definitely didn't have a sense of either. So I knew I didn't have to worry about such a crisis when I decided to leave my successful career. I had accomplished so much. I had helped create and nurture two healthy and thriving children (would become three). I had won the dating lottery relatively early in life when I met my amazing wife and life partner. Then we manufactured a nontraditional retirement lifestyle that we could enjoy at the age of thirty instead of sixty. All while achieving enormous educational and career success by society's standards.

As we neared our retirement, I was on the lookout for another phenomenon that traditionally affects people at the end of their middle-age: The identity crisis of retirement. In a recent episode of the podcast HBR IdeaCast, the Harvard professor Teresa Amabile discusses the implications of identity and retirement.[41] Research has shown that when people are able to answer two important questions favourably, they are much happier in retirement: "Can I afford to retire?" and "Will I be healthy enough to enjoy it?" These were two questions I could easily answer positively.

But Amabile explains that her research at the Harvard Business School is focused on a third equally important set of question that people only tend to ask once they have left the workplace: Who am I now? When people ask me what I do, what do I even tell them? Her preliminary results from a large study on how people transition into retirement, found that, for many, the transition begins smoothly enough but then develops into retirees questioning their own identity and puzzling over how to structure their days as their familiar work life fades into the background.[42]

Many retirees face this type of crisis. And in the ever-growing trend of early retirement, many bloggers are exploring this topic as well. I learned from many writers and podcasters leading up to my own retirement, so I was cognisant of making sure I avoided struggling with my own identity once I gave up my career. I often journaled about this subject in the years leading up to retirement and that really helped. A year before we officially retired, I shared my thoughts with a successful early retirement blog (99to1percent.com). My post really summed up how I felt about my identity. To this day, I still read it regularly and it affirms that I had the right idea. Most of this chapter reflects the thoughts and words I shared back then. The biggest question I contemplated was similar to the ones Teresa Amabile's team researched. I kept thinking of what I would answer when people asked, "What do you do for a living?".

When you think about it, the question "what do you do for a living?" is essentially like asking "what do you do for money?" I always saw this as an inappropriate question that's just been made to sound nicer. It has become a pretty standard and acceptable question in our society and is almost one of the first few questions you ask a person you first meet (after you both point out the obvious weather conditions and lament a little about the current crisis facing our country). In the last year or so before retiring, we had been sharing our plans with more and more people. The fact that we planned on leaving the big city and moving to a small town. The plan to be mortgage free and not work forty hours per week. The idea of spending way more time with our kids and doing the things we love.

Then I got these: "What will you do for a living?" or "How will you make enough money to live?" And then sometimes, "Won't you be bored?"

I knew that what we are doing appeared really strange to most people, but it couldn't have felt any more normal to us. I could explain our plan in detail and sometimes people still assumed we would keep working in our careers but on a part-time basis. The plan, if all went well, was to not work in our current careers. Our jobs were not something we were passionate about. I was good at my job and I earned a good income doing what I did, but it's not something I loved doing, or even liked doing. A likely reality for many of you reading this book. Through the process of building up to our retirement plans I had also realized that my ambitions were far greater than what I could accomplish by working for someone else.

These types of questions stem from the fact that most people draw so much of their identity in their profession (i.e. Doctor, Teacher, Electrician, Accountant etc.) and people just assumed that I would want to hold on to my identity as well. As if I valued some sort of career status. I am very grateful that when it came time to pull the trigger and quit, I had no such desires.

That wasn't always the case though. Ten years ago this type of question would have sounded perfectly logical to me. Whatever changes I would adopt in my life, I could not imagine myself without a career or a job to be proud of. It was part of my identity. I wanted to be known as a successful career man. I wanted to climb the corporate ladder and be a President or a CEO one day.

So, what saved me from an identity crisis? It sounds cliché to say that my kids changed my life, but I can't think of any other reason. When our son was born, a switch went off in my head. All of a sudden, I just didn't see a future as a Vice-President, Director, or President of anything... I thought about this for a long time and came to realize that all I wanted to be known for was being a father and a husband. I figured that it didn't matter if I worked my whole life as a gas station attendant or a successful executive; it didn't mean anything. If I looked back on this life when I was ninety, and I was known as an amazing parent and spouse, I would have lived the exact life I wanted.

So, in essence, the job/career/position didn't matter in my life equation anymore... other than a way to make money to accomplish our greater life goal.

My parents certainly helped in shaping my perspective. They both worked extremely hard their entire life in traditional jobs. But they definitely won't be known for their careers when they are ninety. Their greatest accomplishment and greatest contribution to the world was raising outstanding members of society. Like most people around my age, I also experienced multiple grandparents passing away in the last five years. I even got to see and speak to them many times before they passed. It helped me appreciate the famous quote by Rabbi Harold Kushner when he was referring to what people never say on their deathbed: "I wish I had spent more time at the office".

The fact that nobody wishes they would have spent more time working when they are about to die sounds obvious, but I don't think we truly think about it on a day-to-day basis. In their final palliative moments, my grandparents' focus was their family. They each would have given away all their life savings for another week, day, or even a healthy hour with their children and grandchildren.

I always daydreamed of what my ideal full-time

job would be. What would I do every day with all my time once I quit my job? I correctly imagined I would start by getting up at the same time as I normally do (around 6AM) but that was the only thing that stayed the same. Today, once we are out of bed, we are never in a rush to shower, dress and eat quickly. All while getting the kids dressed and fed while everyone is very cranky. Then stuffing them in the car to make it to daycare/work on time...

On many mornings, I enjoy a peaceful and quiet cup of coffee while I journal and plan what amazing things I would like to accomplish during that day. As with many parents of newborns, our routine was temporarily interrupted for eighteen months because the newest member of our family had decided to start their day between 4AM and 5AM. Eventually she adjusted to a regular sleep schedule and we resumed our morning rituals.

Now when the children wake up, our real "job" (that we love) starts. I make the whole family a great breakfast, we eat together, and we discuss what is on the itinerary for the day. Most of my day is dedicated to giving them as much one-on-one attention as possible. I also don't lose sight of my equally important job of being a husband so making my wife's day special is an important itinerary item daily as well.

So, what do I say when people ask, "what do you do for a living?" I thought of saying something like "I'm a property manager or an entrepreneur...". But the more I thought about it, I didn't like those answers. When I face that exact question, I often answer, "I'm a full-time parent and husband for a living..."

It's not always as easy as it sounds though. I still face lots of skepticism about being a stay-at-home dad. Being the only dad among a dozen moms at the children's playgroup every day likely sparks many thoughts and judgements. I observe common stereotypes every day and was amused by one just the other day. Danielle was hosting a meeting at our house with some members of a volunteer committee she is on and an older lady attending the meeting noticed I was home and playing Play-Doh with my youngest daughter. She approached me and kindly commented that "it must be so nice to be on vacation". I gave a smile and a nod only to realize the implications of the comment later that day. The reality was that the simplest explanation for a man being home with a baby was that I was on vacation. We still live in a world where people cling to stereotypes, but I have learned to happily live with this one.

CHAPTER 17

How to Survive a Financial Crisis

What is a financial crisis?
The American investing and financial education website Investopedia.com defines a financial crisis as a situation when asset prices see a steep decline in value, businesses and consumers are unable to pay their debts, and financial institutions experience liquidity shortages. Contributing factors to a financial crisis include systemic failures, unanticipated or uncontrollable human behavior, incentives to take too much risk, regulatory absence or failures, or contagions that amount to a virus-like spread of problems from one institution or country to the next.[43] The last on the list being the obvious cause of our most recent crisis.

Most people need to be concerned about such crises. Especially those that have retired extremely early and plan on relying on passive investments for the rest of their lives. There have been plenty of financial downturns in the last hundred years, but we suffered through our first one as retirees in 2020 while I was writing this book. With the COVID-19 virus sweeping the world, almost all countries in the world closed their borders. Most countries closed down non-essential businesses and locked in their residents. Every country's economy was forced to slow down to a crawl for six months. This kind of disruption to the world economies inevitably causes a global recession. In just thirty days between late February to late March, the TSX (Canada's Stock Exchange) dropped by 37%. In that same timespan, the New York Stock Exchange dropped by the same amount. Every other stock market in the world also went down by similar amounts.

Many people panicked, thinking the markets would never recover. The outlook did look pretty grim for a while. But what we all needed were reminders that our world economies have gone through many of these drastic downturns and they have always come back. Every single time. People had already forgotten that the last financial recession in 2008 resulted in a much greater fall. From the beginning of the 2008 downturn to its lowest point in March 2009, the Canadian and US stock markets lost over 50% of their value. However, both markets regained their full value within twenty-four months, if you count the dividend yields. That is to say that if someone had not touched their investments in the stock market during the 2008 crash and continued earning dividends, they would have come back to their pre-recession valuation within two years of the lowest point.

The 2008 recession wasn't the only downturn to hit our economies. The 2000 Dot Com crash resulted in North American markets losing about 40% of their value. The 1987 "Black Monday" crash resulted in a single-day 22% drop in Canada and the U.S. Although I don't know anyone who was alive then, who can forget the 1929 depression that wiped out 80% of the TSX. The Great Depression took nearly three years to reach its bottom. But by some accounts, it took less than four and a half years for the stock markets to fully bounce back after the 1929 crisis when you account for the dividends that were still being paid and the fact that the economy experienced drastic deflation.[44] As opposed to inflation when the cost of goods and services goes up, when a country faces deflation, all the prices go down. During the Great Depression, most countries saw huge deflation in prices, which meant that the stock market didn't have to fully recover to the same level to provide comparable market returns.

In every one of these financial downturns, the market always came back and eventually surpassed their pre-crisis peaks. Historically, we seem to suffer a major financial market crash every ten to fifteen years. So as some would say, we were due in 2020.

Any time I have any worries about a financial downturn, I look at quotes from my favorite long-term investor, Warren Buffett, for reassurance. Here is his famous and obvious reflection of the 20th century:

"In the 20th century, the United States endured two world wars and other traumatic and expensive military conflicts; the Depression; a dozen or so recessions and financial panics; oil shocks; a flu epidemic; and the resignation of a disgraced president. Yet the Dow (most commonly followed U.S. stock index) rose from 66 to 11,497."

If anyone had any money to invest in the year 1900 and were warned of all the chaos that would ensue in the next hundred years, they would all run away from the stock market. How can any economy grow, let alone survive under such circumstances? But the reality was that, not only did the economy grow through all this trouble, the human civilization grew by leaps and bounds in almost all measurable statistics. From health, to decreased violence, to overall happiness, we all benefited from the enormous gains that our economies achieved. Someone who invested only $1,000 (approximately $23,000 in 2000 dollars) in the stock market in the year 1900 would have $174,000 in the year 2000. All while supporting an economic system that, although had some flaws, helped bring about the 21st century, which is undeniably the best time to be alive. If you need any proof of this claim, just read Steven Pinker's 2018 book, "Enlightenment Now". In it, Pinker shows that life, health, prosperity, safety, peace, knowledge, and happiness are on the rise, not just in the West, but worldwide.[45]

Now with the worst of the most recent pandemic and financial crisis behind us, I have learned some valuable lessons that I would like to share. We are not completely past this current recession, which may drag out for a few more years, but I have observed one obvious but likely controversial fact: Surviving a financial crisis in retirement is easy... As we will see in this chapter, we survived this financial crisis and actually came out ahead. I will summarize how we survived and thrived during this financial crisis with five critically important rules that may be applicable to all future financial downturns as well.

Rule 1: Don't Panic

When you retire young, much of your wealth will be tied to financial investments. Our wealth is pretty evenly split between financial investments and real estate. Most young investors like us would be wise to focus on more growth-oriented financial portfolios. Growth portfolios focus more on equity or stock market investments. All of our investments are in Vanguard Growth Asset Allocation ETF (VGRO) which holds nearly 80% of its value in the stock market. 30% of those stocks are in the Canadian market, 40% are in the US market and the remaining 30% are in the rest of the world.

As I have discussed in previous chapters, growth portfolios aim for high long-term gains but are much more likely to suffer huge declines during market crashes. Even with financial crashes and drops of 30% to 50% in a single year, a growth portfolio will still generate huge gains in the long term. If you had invested all of your money into a Canadian-based index fund (100% of your money in the Canadian stock market) for forty years from 1979 to 2019 you would have grown your money by an average of 8.8% per year.[46] That is while accounting for three major financial crises during that span, that resulted in drops in the stock markets between 20% and 50% in a single year. Comparatively, the average high-interest savings account offered by big banks today is 1% or less. A very safe bond portfolio generates less than 3% annually.

Now let's compare three scenarios of how a $100,000 investment would grow over forty years.

$100,000 at 8.8% annual growth over 40 years = $2,918,000

$100,000 at 3% annual growth over 40 years = $326,000

$100,000 at 1% annual growth over 40 years = $149,000

So, it's pretty obvious that, although there are risks in investing your money, there may be even greater risks in the long term if you don't. You can be substantially behind the herd financially if you sat on the sidelines for the last forty years.

Before the COVID-19 stock market crash started, we had nearly $500,000 of our net worth tied into the stock market. At its lowest point, we lost almost $150,000. This was just twenty-four months after we quit our jobs and decided to retire. We did have some fears as most people probably did. When you read the headlines at the time, you could have thought you were living a horror movie. We had to remind ourselves that the media will always overestimate bad news, and say things like "this will be the worst financial crisis ever" or "this financial downturn will last much longer than any other". As a society, I think we naturally always assume the worst-case scenarios.

Not only did the financial markets bounce back faster than during any other crash in human history, the markets actually saw overall growth; in a year that was supposed to be worse than the Great Depression. At the time of writing this book, the S&P 500 (U.S. stock market tracking the 500 largest companies) reached a record high. Not a record high for 2020, but an all-time record high. Other stock markets including our own Toronto Stock Exchange saw positive growth in 2020. And when accounting for dividends, most stock markets are ahead of their pre-COVID numbers today. I still can't wrap my mind around this positive story. Instead of coping with a feared retraction of over 40%, our own investment portfolio grew by over 7% in 2020.

Anyone who panicked at the low points of mid to late March and sold off their investments in order to "cut their losses," would realize today the enormity of that mistake. Panicking is never the right answer. From the low point of March 23rd,

2020 when the world seemed at its worst, to November 23rd, 2020, the Canadian stock market grew by over 50% without even accounting for dividend yields. The U.S. stock market grew by an even larger margin. Anyone sitting out during this period, may have lost the equivalent of five years of growth in the span of eight short months.[47] So the key to retiring early is that you are not retiring short term. You are retiring with an extremely long-term horizon. Whatever your plan is, you must look at your finances in terms of a forty or fifty-year outlook. If our net worth goes down during an off year, I know it will come back eventually. We need to avoid panicking and focus on rules 2, 3, 4, and 5 which I will describe next.

Rule 2: Reduce Spending

Reducing spending is an automatic instinct for humans when faced with economic uncertainty. This is a commonly acknowledged fact that has been the subject of many research papers.[48] During the 2008 recession, household spending went down significantly. When the 2020 pandemic market crash occurred, we did like most other households and examined our overall spending to make sure we were not unnecessarily spending, in case this crash was as bad as some predicted.

Unlike most economic recessions, this one was likely a cakewalk when it came to reducing spending. We couldn't travel anymore, we couldn't go out, and we rarely went shopping. This would obviously result in a drop in our overall spending. We had fully planned and paid for a sixty-day West Coast camping trip from May to July. We had budgeted over $4,000 on this trip that would have us visit over a dozen U.S. states and all the provinces to the west of Ontario. This pandemic quickly changed our plans and resulted in way less spending in 2020.

When the schools closed in March, our house got a lot busier, but our grocery bill went down. Making family lunches every day was a lot cheaper than making school lunches. We could avoid buying peanut-free granola bars, cheese strings, and many other individually packed items that made up a large portion of our grocery bill. The increased time spent at home also resulted in savings in other forms when we undertook additional home renovations projects ourselves instead of outsourcing them. We completed a patio stone pathway, a large backyard deck, and refreshed our driveway during the peak of the pandemic.

Rule 3: Take advantage of government stimulus
We have discussed the concept of free money many times in this book. Who doesn't like free money? When the pandemic-related recession started, there seemed to be no shortage of it.

Whether you agree or not with the drastic spending measures the governments undertook when the pandemic started, it is quite a normal occurrence for governments during a financial crisis. During the 2008 financial recession, the Conservative government at the time spent an additional $47 billion over two years to shore up the economy. This resulted in the largest single-year government deficit of $56 billion.[49] At the time, this was considered an absurd amount, but it's almost laughable today. During the pandemic fiscal year of 2020-21 the federal government is estimated to run a deficit of more than $343 billion.[50]

In just the first twelve months of the pandemic, as part of the various government spendings we will receive nearly $5,000 in additional benefits. The federal government gave every parent in the country a one-time payment of $300 per child in 2020. And then announced an additional $1,200 for every child under six in 2021 for families with a household income under $120,000. Additionally, our provincial government has given out $400 per child during the pandemic so far. As I mentioned earlier, since our spending actually went down during this period, these payments strictly added to our savings.

The governments also provided additional financial benefits to most seniors who were traditionally retired as well as financial benefits for nearly every segment of the population that would have had their employment affected. If you had just decided to pursue a semi-retired lifestyle and gave up a secure career but then suddenly lost your gig-economy job or otherwise part-time income source when the pandemic started, you were also protected. The CERB (Canada Emergency Response Benefit) was very generous and helped most people that saw a reduction in their income.

All this does not discount the fact that this financial crisis and pandemic was difficult financially on some people. But as we can see in this chapter, with the help of an abundance of government support, this crisis was definitely survivable. Even for those like us that have given up their traditional primary source of income and retired extremely early.

Rule 4: Make money if you have to
Danielle and I were business graduates, so we had plenty of experience making business plans. When we decided that we wanted to pursue an extremely early retirement, we naturally made a business plan. We created pro forma financial statements (a projection-based financial analysis) with worst-case and best-case scenarios. We even outlined the potential threats to our retirement plan as well as remedies to those threats. It

doesn't have to be a forty-page document with graphs and tables like ours, but doing this exercise is a good idea for anyone looking to retire early. One of the biggest threats to our plan was a potential financial crisis. We had not identified increased government benefits as a remedy to this threat, so we were pleasantly surprised to receive a financial boost even during a period that we did not need it. Our biggest shield to a financial crisis was always to just go out and make money.

If all our investments suffered substantially and we found ourselves with a reduced or temporarily eliminated income source, we would first adopt Rule 1: Don't Panic. Then we would appreciate the fact that we have such a low-cost lifestyle. Our greatest strength has never been the fact that we amassed a sizable net worth or our careers' successes. Our greatest strength has been our ability to live a great life for less. Knowing that in a worst-case scenario we would simply need to generate $30,000 for ourselves while the world figured itself out and our investments would come back to normal was not a very daunting task. As we now know, we didn't have to adopt this rule, but looking back we don't think we would have had much trouble doing so.

General labour was a great example of such an opportunity during this particular financial crisis.

During the summer of 2020, the local contractors in our small town could not keep up with the demand. With nowhere to go on vacation or otherwise go spend their money, our economies saw a boom in renovation and construction services. Being somewhat handy, I could have taken a number of construction jobs for six months in order to pay our living expenses for the following year. It may sound overly simplistic to say this but there seems to always be work available to those who are willing to take it. It won't always be at your education level, skill level, or even compensate you for what you think you deserve. But most of the time, if your worst-case scenario occurs, there will be work there if you need to supplement your income temporarily.

Rule 5: Reassess
As I mentioned earlier, we have two main sources of wealth: our real estate properties and our financial investments. Many people retire and rely solely on their financial investment by living on 3% or 4% of their investments. Our strategy was different and much safer. We will not be relying on our financial investments until we are in our fifties. Our financial investments were sort of a safety net, only to be used once we no longer wanted to manage our real estate properties.

During a financial crisis, it is wise to re-examine

your financial plans in life. In doing so, we came up with a plan to drastically increase our net worth, simplify our life, and provide even more financial security. In the midst of the 2020 recession, many real estate markets saw huge growth. My presumption was that people were more wary of the stock markets than ever, so there was more demand for physical investments such as real estate. Also, many people were reassessing their living situations. For example, if you can work from home, maybe you no longer need to live so close to work. People may have also seen a certain value in moving to smaller towns because they were less affected by the risk of the virus and the ensuing restrictions. In our own small town, we started seeing houses and apartment buildings go on the market and be listed as sold within days. Additionally, the overall supply of properties for sale was extremely low, which meant that the demand was high.

When we examined our finances for the last two years, we saw that we could afford to lose the cash flow of one of our income properties and still maintain our standard of living. We decided to look into unlocking the value in one of our real estate properties and shifting it to our long-term savings. This would allow us to divest more of our money to a purely passive form of investment. In turn, it would result in less management and even more time to be a parent and pursue our hobbies. Due to our constant analysis of the market and financial situation, we were able to take advantage of a quick sale. We were able to turn a significant profit on a property we had owned for just three years.

We had only been retired two years when 2020 presented us with a massive curveball. The biggest threat to our plans was in front of us. But by applying our five rules, we not only survived this financial crisis, but we also had one of our best years yet. In 2020, we finally surpassed a net worth of $1 million. This was a subtle milestone we had set for ourselves when we retired in 2018. We never imagined that it would occur so quickly, and certainly not during our first financial recession.

CONCLUSION

You've made it to the end of the book. I hope you drew some inspiration from our story and gained some knowledge to help you on your journey. As the title of the book prefaced, this was intended to be a guide to help you achieve an earlier retirement. Now, more than ever, I think people need to take their retirement plans very seriously for two specific reasons. The first is that most people don't love their jobs. One recent survey of Canadians showed that only about one quarter reported actually being satisfied with their job. Some of the big reasons cited were that people didn't find their work interesting and many people just didn't see how their work made a difference.[51] The second reason is to free yourself from the financial obligation of a traditional job. It's not a topic that many like to discuss, but most Canadians don't currently have a choice but to go to work. One 2017 study revealed that 47% of Canadians said it would be difficult to meet their financial obligations if their paycheck was delayed by just a single week.[52] By aiming for early retirement, you build a financial cushion on the way. You become less tied to a job you don't like, and you steer further away from a paycheck-to-paycheck lifestyle.

I certainly felt this liberty right from the beginning of our journey. Even before reaching our actual goal, we enjoyed so much more freedom by having our finances in order. Having financial breathing room allowed us to take more risks in our careers and we were able to take much bigger risks in our real estate investments. Our marriage also benefited from having a solid financial plan. Some studies have identified disagreements over finances as one of the top reasons couples seek marital counseling, as well as one of the top reasons for divorce.[53] I can honestly say that my wife and I have never had an argument over money, other than deciding if we should spend $10 on each other at Christmas or $20. (This is actually a fun exercise and forces you to be creative and thoughtful to make your money go the furthest.)

We are nearly three years into our retirement journey and we luckily have not had the chance to be bored yet. I haven't binge watched a single Netflix series during the day yet. I haven't yet indulged in a feared video game addiction. Other than spending a few hours last Saturday helping my son beat Bowser in World Three of Super Mario on his Nintendo DS (when we finally did it, the victory felt just as good as I remembered it twenty years ago). All these habits are very difficult to pick up since we haven't owned a television in almost four years.

Retirement has given us the gift of time. The time to truly do all the things we want to do and the time to take care of our health. When I worked full-time, I tried to exercise regularly and would often successfully get into a routine. But as soon as life got too busy, I would sacrifice that routine and not regain it for months. Now, life literally cannot get "too busy". So, I have been able to stick to a consistent workout routine for over two years. Time has also allowed me to incorporate yoga and meditation in my daily life. I've had the time to sit down at least a few mornings per week to create this book for the last year. I had time to become a kid again and to build a backyard ice rink and 8-foot-high snow fort. As I have documented repeatedly in this book, the benefits have been endless.

I'd like to end this book with one obvious fact that you may have thought to yourself throughout this book: I am not special. Just like my idols Pete Adeney (Mr. Money Mustache) and Jacob Lund Fisker (Early Retirement Extreme) are not special. The story I shared is not particularly special. It definitely is special to me but not remarkable by any means. It's just an account that shows that you don't have to follow the norms. You don't have to stick with the status quo and work for thirty-five years in order to finally enjoy life. It all starts with a plan.

ACKNOWLEDGEMENTS

While writing this book I often thought about what I would write in this section. I've been reading nearly fifty books per year since retiring and always read the acknowledgment section. I truly think it's one of the most important parts of the book. A book often has only one author but sometimes others contribute enormously, and you get an opportunity to know them just a little in the acknowledgements.

In my case, you should all get to know my wife, life partner, and best friend, Danielle. She was not only instrumental in creating this book, but even more so in creating this story. I truly can't imagine being able to achieve early retirement without her as a partner. Her ambitions matched my own and her wisdom and patience complemented my passion and stubbornness. From re-reading and editing every word I wrote, to spending countless hours listening and dissecting my ideas, she helped bring this book to life. I am eternally grateful.

There are other people who were also extremely important in the production of this book. Thanks to Celestian Rice for his editing services. And thanks to Ben Theoret and Diane Therrien who generously volunteered their time to pre-read my book multiple times to provide enormously important feedback along the way.

This next part will sound extremely cheesy since I may be thanking someone who might never read my book. But out of all the authors, celebrities or athletes I have followed or looked up to in my life, I don't think a single one came close to the impact Mr. Money Mustache had on my life trajectory. There is just something about his writing from the very beginning that resonated with me and helped me see a vision to a much better life. So, thanks Pete if you ever read this book.

Lastly, although I cannot thank them for being born, I will express my gratitude to my children who gave me the best job in the entire world: Dad.

ABOUT THE AUTHOR

Réjean Venne worked in the insurance industry for eight years before retiring at twenty-nine. Ambitious career goals as well as smart saving and investment strategies allowed him to leave a big-city job and become a full-time parent. Réjean and his wife Danielle, along with their three young children, live in Sturgeon Falls, Ontario. They write regularly on topics related to parenting, health, mindfulness, and money. You can follow them at www.mindfulfamily.ca or email them at mindfulfamilyvenne@gmail.com.

NOTES

Introduction
(1) McGugan, Ian. "How to Retire at Age 30 (and Stay Retired)." The Globe and Mail, 2 Apr. 2015, www.theglobeandmail.com/globe-investor/retirement/retire-planning/how-to-retire-at-age-30/article23778559/.

Chapter 1
(2) Dominguez, J. R., & Robin, V. (1992). Your money or your life: Transforming your relationship with money and achieving financial independence. New York: Viking.

(3) Cooley, Philip L.; Hubbard, Carl M.; Walz, Daniel T. (1998). "Retirement Savings: Choosing a Withdrawal Rate That Is Sustainable" (PDF). AAII Journal. 10(3): 16–21

(4) Mr. Money Mustache. The Shockingly Simple Math Behind Early Retirement. 13 June 2012, www.mrmoneymustache.com/2012/01/13/the-shockingly-sim-

ple-math-behind-early-retirement/.

(5) Fisker, Jacob Lund. Early Retirement Extreme: A Philosphical and Practical Guide to Financial Independence. CreateSpace, 2010.

Chapter 2
(6) Urban, Tim. "The Tail End." Wait But Why, 11 Dec. 2015, waitbutwhy.com/2015/12/the-tail-end.html.

Chapter 3
(7) Housel, Morgan. The Psychology of Money. Jaico Publishing, 2020.

Chapter 5
(8) David Richter, Michael D Krämer, Nicole K Y Tang, Hawley E Montgomery-Downs, Sakari Lemola, Long-term effects of pregnancy and childbirth on sleep satisfaction and duration of first-time and experienced mothers and fathers, Sleep, Volume 42, Issue 4, April 2019, zsz015, https://doi.org/10.1093/sleep/zsz015

(9) Haaland , Mary. "Being a Mom Is the Equivalent of 2.5 Full-Time Jobs, According to Survey." New York Post, New York Post, 7 May 2019, nypost.com/2019/05/07/being-a-mom-is-the-equivalent-of-2-5-full-time-jobs-according-to-survey/.

(10) "Study Reveals Highest and Lowest Child Care Fees in Canadian Cities in 2018." Canadian Centre for Policy Alternatives, 7 Feb. 2019, www.policyalternatives.ca/newsroom/news-releases/study-reveals-highest-and-lowest-child-care-fees-canadian-cities-2018.

Chapter 6

(11) "The Average Price of a Detached Home in Toronto Is Now over $1.5 Million." BlogTO, BlogTO, 17 Sept. 2020, www.blogto.com/real-estate-toronto/2020/09/average-price-detached-home-toronto-1-5-million/.

(12) "Vancouver Detached Home Prices Are Flat, Even With A 24% Jump In Sales." Better Dwelling, 8 Apr. 2020, betterdwelling.com/city/vancouver/vancouver-detached-home-prices-are-flat-even-with-a-24-jump-in-sales/.

(13) "Ottawa Real Estate Board." Ottawa Real Estate Board Median Price | CREA Statistics, 2020, creastats.crea.ca/mls/otta-median-price/.

(14) Uppal, Sharanjit. Homeownership, Mortgage Debt and Types of Mortgage among Canadian Families. Government of Canada, Statistics Canada, 8 Aug. 2019, www150.statcan.gc.ca/n1/pub/75-006-x/2019001/article/00012-eng.htm.

(15) Mortgage and Consumer Credit Trends: Q4 2018, Canada Mortgage and Housing Corporation, 22 May 2019, www.cmhc-schl.gc.ca/en/housing-observer-online/2019-housing-observer/mortgage-consumer-credit-trends-q4-2018.

(16) "National Price Map." CREA, Sept. 2020, www.crea.ca/housing-market-stats/national-price-map/.

(17) Brownell, Claire. "Canada's Best Places to Live for Low Taxes: Top 100 Cities." MoneySense, 31 July 2018, www.moneysense.ca/spend/real-estate/best-places-to-live-in-canada-low-taxes-2018-100/.

Chapter 7
(18) Government of Canada, Statistics Canada. "Survey of Household Spending, 2017." The Daily, 12 Dec. 2018, www150.statcan.gc.ca/n1/daily-quotidien/181212/dq181212a-eng.htm.

(19) Toups, Des. "How Many Times Will You Crash Your Car?" Forbes, Forbes Magazine, 27 July 2011, www.forbes.com/sites/moneybuilder/2011/07/27/how-many-times-will-you-crash-your-car/.

Chapter 8
(20) Detailed Food Spending, Canada, Regions and Provinces, Government of Canada, Statistics Can-

ada, 12 Dec. 2018, www150.statcan.gc.ca/t1/tbl1/en/tv.action?pid=1110012501.

Chapter 9
(21) "Canadian Lottery: Sales by Province or Territory 2019." Statista, 1 Apr. 2020, www.statista.com/statistics/388346/sales-of-lotteries-by-province-canada/.

(22) "Lottery Players Fact Sheet." About OLG, 31 Dec. 2019, about.olg.ca/news-information/lottery-players-fact-sheet/.

Chapter 10
(23) "The Best Time To Buy And Sell A Used Car: Understanding Depreciation." RideTime.ca, 20 Feb. 2018, www.ridetime.ca/blog/the-best-time-to-buy-and-sell-a-used-car-understanding-depreciation/.

(24) "Employer Pension Plans (Trusteed Pension Funds), Third Quarter 2016." Statistics Canada, 17 Mar. 2017, www.benefitscanada.com/wp-content/uploads/2017/03/StatsCan_Pension-Plans_Q22016.pdf.

(25) Central Government Debt. Government of Canada, Statistics Canada, 2 Dec. 2020, www150.statcan.gc.ca/t1/tbl1/en/tv.action?pid=1010000201.

(26) BMO Financial Group. "BMO 10th Annual RRSP Study: Canadians RRSP Savings on the Rise but Still Struggle to Define Retirement Financial Goals." Cision in Canada, 6 Feb. 2020, www.newswire.ca/news-releases/bmo-10th-annual-rrsp-study-canadians-rrsp-savings-on-the-rise-but-still-struggle-to-define-retirement-financial-goals-823178017.html.

(27) Ardrey, Matthew. "Taking a Pension's Commuted Value Can Leave Some Canadians Wealthier." The Globe and Mail, 31 Aug. 2020, www.theglobeandmail.com/investing/globe-advisor/advisor-news/article-taking-a-pensions-commuted-value-can-leave-some-canadians-wealthier/.

Chapter 11
(28) "Compound Interest." Wikipedia, Wikimedia Foundation, 15 Nov. 2020, en.m.wikipedia.org/wiki/Compound_interest.

(29) Mr. Money Mustache. "What I'm Teaching My Son about Money.", 20 May 2015, www.mrmoneymustache.com/2015/05/20/what-im-teaching-my-son-about-money/.

(30) Financial Consumer Agency of Canada. "Payday Loans." Canada.ca, Government of Canada, 15 May 2020, www.canada.ca/en/financial-consumer-agency/services/loans/payday-loans.html.

(31) Financial Consumer Agency of Canada. "Payday Loans: Market Trends." Canada.ca, Government of Canada, 28 Apr. 2017, www.canada.ca/en/financial-consumer-agency.html.

(32) "Canadians Carrying Fewer Credit Cards, but Higher Balances." CBC News, CBC/Radio Canada, 8 Mar. 2017, www.cbc.ca/news/business/canada-credit-cards-transunion-1.4015250.

(33) Brown, Jordann. "What Happens If I Only Make the Minimum Credit Card Payment?" Ratehub.ca, 5 June 2020, www.ratehub.ca/blog/credit-card-minimum-payment-explainer/.

Chapter 13
(34) Hayes, Adam. "Understanding Perfect Competition." Investopedia, 1 July 2020, www.investopedia.com/terms/p/perfect-competition.asp.

(35) Elkins, Kathleen. "Warren Buffett: Most People Shouldn't Pick Individual Stocks-Here's How to Invest Instead." CNBC, CNBC, 22 May 2020, www.cnbc.com/2020/05/22/warren-buffett-most-people-shouldnt-pick-single-stocks.html.

(36) Fast Facts about Vanguard, about.vanguard.com/who-we-are/fast-facts/.

(37) "Getting Started." Canadian Couch Potato, canadiancouchpotato.com/getting-started/.

Chapter 14
(38) "Child and Family Benefits Calculator." Canada.ca, Canada Revenue Agency, 1 Apr. 2016, www.canada.ca/en/revenue-agency/services/child-family-benefits/child-family-benefits-calculator.html.

Chapter 15
(39) Valérie, Ouellet. "40% Of Ontario Full-Time Post-Secondary Students Granted Free Tuition, CBC Analysis Shows | CBC News." CBCnews, CBC/Radio Canada, 4 Feb. 2019, www.cbc.ca/news/canada/toronto/ontario-schools-tuition-data-1.5003005.

(40) Government of Canada, Statistics Canada. "Tuition Fees for Degree Programs, 2019/2020." The Daily;, 4 Sept. 2019, www150.statcan.gc.ca/n1/daily-quotidien/190904/dq190904b-eng.htm.

Chapter 16
(41) "HBR IdeaCast Episode 665: How Retirement Changes Your Identity." Harvard Business Review, 15 Jan. 2019, hbr.org/podcast/2019/01/how-retirement-changes-your-identity.

(42) Gerdeman, Dina. "Welcome to Retirement. Who Am I Now?" HBS Working Knowledge, 17 Sept. 2018, hbswk.hbs.edu/item/welcome-to-retirement-who-am-i-now.

Chapter 17
(43) Kenton, Will. "Financial Crisis." Investopedia, Investopedia, 16 Mar. 2020, www.investopedia.com/terms/f/financial-crisis.asp.

(44) Hulbert, Mark. "25 Years to Bounce Back? Try 4½." The New York Times, The New York Times, 25 Apr. 2009, www.nytimes.com/2009/04/26/your-money/stocks-and-bonds/26stra.html.

(45) Pinker, Steven, Enlightenment Now. Penguin-RandomHouse, 2018

(46) TaxTips.ca. "Historical Returns on Stock Market and Other Investments." TaxTips.ca, 28 Oct. 2020, www.taxtips.ca/stocksandbonds/investmentreturns.htm.

(47) "Google Finance - Stock Market Prices, Real-Time Quotes & Business News." Google, Google, www.google.com/finance.

(48) Petev, Ivaylo D, and Luigi Pistaferri. "Consumption in the Great Recession." The Russell Sage Foundation and The Stanford Center on Poverty and Inequality, Oct. 2012,

doi:https://inequality.stanford.edu/sites/default/files/Consumption_fact_sheet.pdf.

(49) Curry, Bill, and Barrie McKenna. "Stimulus Gamble: How Ottawa Saved the Economy – and Wasted Billions." The Globe and Mail, 8 Feb. 2014, www.theglobeandmail.com/report-on-business/stimulus-gamble-how-ottawa-saved-the-economy-and-wasted-billions/article16760149/.

(50) Di Matteo, Livio. "BLOG: Canada's Fiscal Situation near Crisis Levels." Fraser Institute, 24 Nov. 2020, www.fraserinstitute.org/blogs/canadas-fiscal-situation-near-crisis-levels?language=en.

Conclusion

(51) Montgomery, Marc. "Only about One Quarter of Canadians Satisfied with Their Job." RCI, Radio Canada International, 17 Dec. 2018, www.rcinet.ca/en/2018/12/17/only-about-one-quarter-of-canadians-satisfied-with-their-job/.

(52) The Canadian Press. "47% Of Canadians Living Paycheque to Paycheque, Survey Finds - BNN Bloomberg." BNN, 6 Sept. 2017, www.bnnbloomberg.ca/47-of-canadians-living-paycheque-to-paycheque-survey-finds-1.848429.

(53) Ni, Preston. "7 Keys to Long-Term Relationship Success." Psychology Today, Sussex Publishers, 7 Oct. 2012, www.

psychologytoday.com/ca/blog/communication-success/201210/7-keys-long-term-relationship-success.

Manufactured by Amazon.ca
Acheson, AB